BLOCK ISL

HISTORY, PROCESSES AND FIELD EXCURSIONS

BY

LES SIRKIN

Published by:

BOOK & TACKLE SHOP
7 Bay Street
Watch Hill, R.I. 02891
401-596-0700

To the people of Block Island for
preserving their environment.

THE
BOOK
&
TACKLE
SHOP
Established
1953

COPYRIGHT © 1994 by LES SIRKIN.

Sole Distributor:

BOOK & TACKLE SHOP
7 Bay Street
Watch Hill, R.I. 02891
401-596-0700

ISBN Number 0-910258-20-1
Printed in the United States of America
Entire contents ©

Table of Contents

List of Illustrations

1

2

BLOCK ISLAND GEOLOGY: HISTORY AND PROCESSES

INTRODUCTION

Although we are only twelve miles from the mainland, we somehow feel close to nature on Block Island. The physical world makes its presence known directly through the dynamics of the atmosphere and the ocean, especially when the wind and the sea rise, rain drives against the land, and our plans are disrupted.

In contrast, geological processes are set in a different time frame and are much less imposing on a short-term basis. The erosive forces of wind and waves seem to be tempered in only a few hours; the bluffs retain their profiles, even though the slopes have deeper gullies, and the beaches are intact, but with step-like terraces tracing their seaward margins. Geologically, the elongation of Sandy Point proceeds unnoticed. But from the perspective of geologic processes and time, the Island has changed dramatically since twenty-two thousand years ago when the Laurentide ice sheet covered eastern North America between northern Canada and southern New England and New York. Because of this glaciation, Block

Island formed like a dot of icing on the top of a geologic layer cake. The Island today is a small mass of gravel sitting above layers of clay and sand, all of which are piled on a basement complex of crystalline bedrock.

The geology of Block Island can be best understood in the context of the history of the earth's crust, which traces the formation and movements of the continents. In the succeeding chapters we will consider this history, beginning with the origin of the bedrock foundation of northeastern North America (Figure 1). This segment of the continent began to evolve in the Proterozoic Era over one billion years ago. At that time the precambrian shield, largely of Archean age, the most ancient part of the emerging North American continent, which has segments that date to nearly four billion years, collided with another, equally ancient crustal fragment. The rocks that formed the margins of these continents were crumpled and metamorphosed, and a massive mountain range was created. With an age of deformation of about one billion years, these metamorphic rocks are the oldest in the core of the southern New England upland. This collision was followed by an interval of rifting apart of these continents and

ERAS	PERIODS	AGE (my*)	EVENTS
Cenozoic	Quaternary	0 to 2	Cyclic glaciation (see Figure 10)
	Tertiary	2 to 65	Northern Hemisphere glaciation; Erosion of S.New England upland.
Mesozoic	Cretaceous	65-144	Continents move toward modern positions;Buildup of continental shelf.
	Jurassic	144-213	Pangaea begins to split apart 200my;Basins form.
	Triassic	213-248	
Paleozoic	Permian	248-286	Pangaea Supercontinent completed;Appalachian Mts completed.
	Pennsylvanian	286-320	Coal swamps form
	Mississippian	320-360	
	Devonian	360-408	Laurasia and Gondwana begin to merge.
	Silurian	408-438	
	Ordovician	438-505	Laurasian continents begin to merge.
	Cambrian	505-590	Avalonia joins N.A.
Proterozoic		590-2500	Protocontinents develop
Archean		2500-4600	Beginning of Planet Earth,4600my

Figure 1.   The Geologic Time Scale (0 to 4.6 billion years ago; my*
= ages in million years). For Quaternary Time Scale see
Figure 10).

Figure 1.

opening of the ocean basin. As the continents separated in late Proterozoic time, a thick layer of sediment was deposited on the margin of proto- North America.

The next part of this history traces the growth of the Appalachian Mountain chain during the Paleozoic Era from nearly six hundred million years ago to about two hundred fifty million years ago. These mountains were also the result of an episode of continental collisions. This time the crustal plates of ancestral North America, Europe and Africa ground against each other (Figure 2). Again, the sedimentary rocks of the margins of the continents were transformed into mountain ranges.

The process was reversed during the Mesozoic Era, around two hundred million years ago when the supercontinent, made up of all of the existing continents, began to break apart, and the Atlantic ocean basin formed in the widening rift. Sediment from the erosion of the Paleozoic mountains built a new sedimentary margin on the North American continent. By the end of the Cretaceous Period around sixty-five million years ago, a wedge of sediment had been deposited seaward from the foothills of the Appalachians to the edge of the continental shelf. This mass of stratified

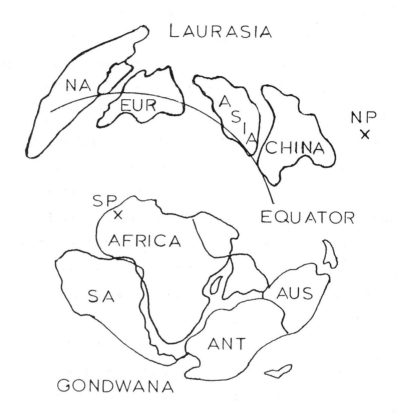

Figure 2. Relative positions of the mid-Paleozoic continents with near-modern outlines for location.

sediments rests unconformably on the crystalline rock of the Paleozoic-age basement (Figure 3b).

How Block Island got on top of the pile is the subject of the third component of the book. The glaciers of the Pleistocene Epoch were responsible for transporting and depositing a vast quantity of sediment at their outermost margins to form a narrow zone of hills, known as moraines. The terminal moraine and the recessional moraines of this glaciation run through Long Island, Block Island, Martha's Vineyard and Nantucket (Figure 4). Twice during the last two hundred thousand years, the continental glaciers expanded southward and deposited moraines in virtually the same region. The last ice, which arrived some twenty-two thousand years ago, created the rough stock from which the offshore islands would be carved by subsequent geologic forces.

The last part of this geologic history deals with the transformation of the moraines by the erosive action of ocean currents and a rising sea, as well as by wind, rainfall and surface streams. All of these erosional forces have contributed to the present size and shape of Block Island. The glaciations and the postglacial geological processes are the most dramatic of the

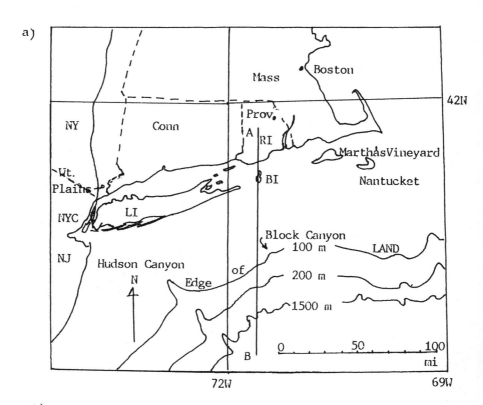

a)

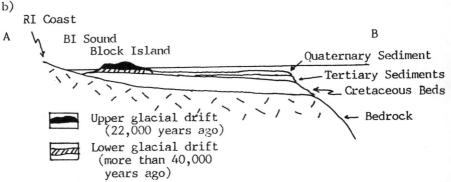

b)

Figure 3a.   The southern New England coast and continental shelf, and the edge of land at the maximum of the last glaciation, 22,000 years ago.

3b.   An idealized cross section of the continental shelf along line AB in Figure 3a. Vertical not to scale.

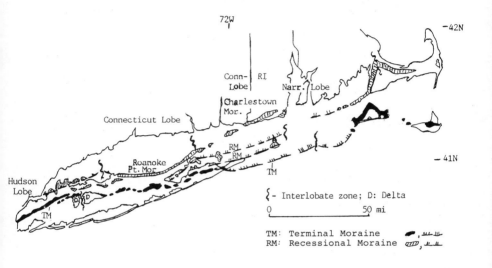

Figure 4. Late Wisconsinan moraines and glacial lobes of 20,000 to 22,000 years ago in southern New England and New York.

chapters of this history because they created the Island as we see it, and because we can study their effects firsthand.

During the last glaciation, the Laurentide ice sheet, named for its source region in eastern Canada, covered southern New England. The ice tapered southward to the outermost range of glacial deposits, the terminal moraine, just south of where Block Island stands today. The shoreline of the Atlantic Ocean was seventy miles south of the ice front and near the edge of the continental shelf, and the sea was over three hundred fifty feet below its present level. Rivers cut canyons into the shelf where ice-age mammals grazed over land covered with tundra and spruce forests (Figure 3b). The terminal moraine, itself, is a massive deposit of sand and gravel that marks the outer limits of the ice (Figure 4). When the glacier began to melt and the ice front receded northward, recessional moraines formed along temporary ice margins as secondary ridges on the southern New England landscape.

The changes imposed on the surface as the glacier melted and began to replenish the ocean are also very impressive. If we had been able to see Block Island twelve thousand years ago when the sea was within one hundred feet of its present level, it would have appeared like a rounded diamond and about three times bigger than it is today (Figure 5). We would also have witnessed meltwater accumulating between the glacier and the terminal moraine and flooding the valleys of the mainland. As the water spilled over the moraine from the outlets of vast freshwater glacial lakes that stood where Long Island Sound and Block Island Sound are today, ocean currents undercut the moraine allowing the impounded water to sluice through the gaps and into the sea. The streams rushing from the lakes carved broad and deep channels that exist today through the moraine and across the sea floor. Ultimately, the rising sea flooded the lake basins and surrounded the surviving highlands of the moraines.

Six thousand years ago when sea level approached its present level, Block Island stood as two islands with prominent ridges separated by a glacial channel where Great Salt Pond lies today. From that time onward, the Island has gradually been modified, downsized and streamlined by geologic processes. Coastal processes have connected the two postglacial islands with barrier

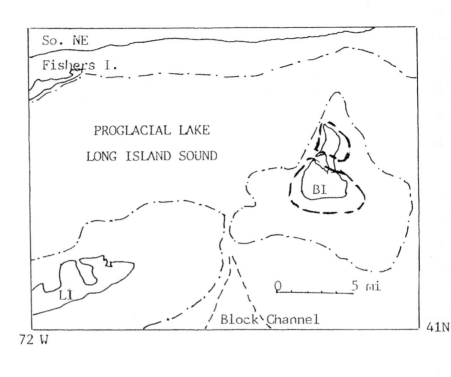

So. NE

Fishers I.

PROGLACIAL LAKE

LONG ISLAND SOUND

BI

0   5 mi

LI

Block Channel

72 W

41N

_._._ 12,000 years ago

__ __ 6,000 years ago- Block Island

_____ At present

Figure 5. Rhode Island shelf shorelines 12,000 and 6000 years ago.

beaches, creating the Island in the form we know. Rain, wind and waves have torn away at the land, and rainfall has saturated the glacial sediments to create a water table. More recently people have arrived bringing their own style of modifying nature. What we can see of Block Island today is the product of many geological processes. These processes and the rising sea are continuing to reshape the Island, steadily releasing its treasure of sediment into the encroaching sea with the probability of creating as dramatic changes in the future as have occurred in the past.

The story of this island, its geological history and the processes that are at work are the subjects of this book. Field excursions are provided to enable direct examination of the prominent geological features and processes that are discussed herein.

GEOLOGIC HISTORY

BUILDING THE CONTINENTS

Beginning early in the earth's history four billion years ago, fragments of the earliest crust were merging to form continent-sized land masses. These fragments included the first volcanic islands and deposits of volcanic debris that formed over rifts in the hardened surface of the planet. Through the Archean and Proterozoic eras, these protocontinents acquired a history of growth through numerous collisions and separations of crustal fragments of increasing size and complexity (Figure 1).

Early in the Paleozoic Era, over five hundred million years ago, two major continents, Laurasia and Gondwana, were taking shape, incorporating most of the available continental crust (Figure 2). Laurasia grew from the merging of the continental blocks that would eventually become North America, Europe and Asia, along with some large volcanic island arcs and adjoining basin complexes, features that probably resembled the present islands of Japan and the Sea of Japan. The rocks of one of these island-basin features, known as Avalonia, make up part of easternmost New England. The components of Laurasia merged, beginning in early Paleozoic time, forming mountain ranges like the Ural Mountains between Europe and Asia, and the Appalachians between Europe and North America. The suture between ancestral North America and Europe can be found near the New York-Connecticut border. The continental margin where Block Island would eventually form would not begin to emerge for another three hundred million years (Figure 3b). Unlike North America in our modern geography, Laurasia was aligned with the equator in the area of eastern North America where the Appalachian Mountains are today. This region supported tropical climate from what is now Georgia to Northern Canada.

The other early Paleozoic continent, Gondwana, was mainly in the southern hemisphere and combined crustal elements ancestral to Africa, South America, India, Australia, and the Antarctic (Figure 2). Laurasia and Gondwana gradually collided, beginning in the middle of the Devonian Period around three hundred eighty million years ago and ending late in the Permian Period about two hundred fifty million years ago, to create the ultimate supercontinent, Pangaea, a fusing of virtually all of the continental crust on earth at that time (Figure 6). Pangaea remained intact until the end of the Triassic Period of the Mesozoic Era, two hundred million years ago.

Both continental crust and oceanic crust were involved in these collisions, and pieces of oceanic crust were often trapped between continents. Usually lighter continental crust overrode heavier oceanic rock which plunged deep into the earth forming a subduction zone (Figure 7). Occasionally slices of oceanic crust were shoved onto the continent in a process known as obduction. The heat generated in these movements melted continental rock above the subduction zone creating masses of molten rock called magma. Under pressure the magma was forced upward in the continental crust and slowly crystallized into mountain-sized bodies of granitic rock known as batholiths. Later, magma from oceanic crust was injected through the crust to form veins of basalt in the existing bedrock and volcanoes and lava flows at the surface. The older continental crust was altered by the heat and pressure of the molten intrusions into crystalline metamorphic rock, known as gneiss and schist. These rocks contain a mix of minerals

Figure 6. The supercontinent, Pangaea, at the end of the Paleozoic, with near-modern continental outlines for location.

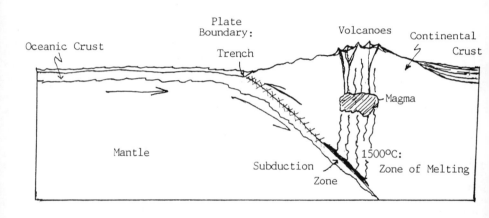

Figure 7. Cross section of an oceanic crust- continental
crust collision and the formation of a subduction zone.

arranged in light and dark bands that reveal their continental and oceanic sources.

The modern interactions between Australia, India, Asia, and the volcanic island arcs and basins of the Pacific provide models for the Paleozoic crustal collisions. The collision-in-progress between Australia and Asia is an approximation of the collision between Gondwana and Laurasia. Similarly, the merging of India and Asia during the Cenozoic Era has resulted in the building of the Himalayan Mountains out of the marine sedimentary rocks compressed between these continents. This is a modern analog of the late stage in the Paleozoic collisions that formed the Appalachian Mountains. From these models we can understand the development of the continents that now border the Atlantic Ocean, and we can reconstruct the collisions and compression of continental and oceanic crust and the thick sedimentary layers that created the mountain ranges of the Paleozoic Era.

Today, southern New England contains the roots of these mountains and includes leftover pieces of Eurasia and Gondwana. Granitic intrusions fringe southern Rhode Island and Connecticut, and gneisses and schists make up much of the interior. In addition, darker basaltic rocks stretch northward through central Rhode Island, perhaps representing oceanic crust caught between the continents.

As Pangaea neared completion late in the Paleozoic Era, an elongated embayment formed where the Narragansett Bay lowland now lies. An arm of the late Paleozoic ocean occupied this trough and coarse gravels were washed into the bay by rivers from nearby mountains. These gravels were soon converted to conglomerates, a type of sedimentary rock made of cemented rock debris. Crustal forces later changed these rocks into metaconglomerates in which the pebbles were stretched and the sandy matrix crystallized. In swamps around the quiet waters of the bay, the remains of forests of primitive trees were ultimately transformed into beds of coal.

At the end of the Paleozoic Era, Pangaea stood firm with the Appalachian Mountains as its backbone. Southern New England, including the present position of Block Island, was buried under thousands of feet of crustal rock. This landmass remained intact for tens of millions of years, well into the early Mesozoic.

As the Triassic Period ended, two hundred million years ago, Pangaea began to split apart, literally at its

Paleozoic seams. Sheets of lava were extruded from rifts that opened like torn cloth at the edges of the new continents. These events appear to be similar to the rifting that is underway in eastern Africa today. Deep valleys, now known as Mesozoic basins, formed in the rifted depressions of eastern North America. Streams eroded the nearby uplands and carried oxidized sediments that would become red sandstone into the basins, while black lavas flowed over the sandstone layers. The Mesozoic basins were probably similar to the modern Red Sea basin between Africa and Arabia.

This continent-splitting cataclysm created several basins, including the Hartford Basin which is now occupied by the Connecticut River Valley (Figure 8). Here red and brown sandstones are capped by basaltic lava flows that form cliffs along the valley. Other rifts are buried in the continental shelf, and one of these lies south of Block Island. The Newark Basin of eastern New Jersey is wedged between the Appalachians and the Atlantic coastal plain. The breaking of the earth's crust into large blocks, or plates, and movement of these plates, made possible by the softening of the rock beneath the continents, coupled with the circular,

a)

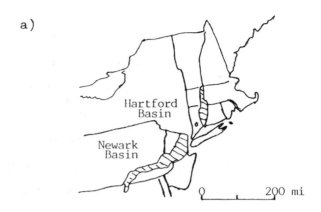

Hartford
Basin

Newark
Basin

0 _____ 200 mi

b)

lava Flow

Sill

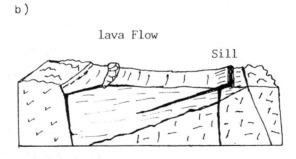

Figure 8a. Mesozoic basins from southern New England to
New Jersey.
    8b. A block diagram of a Mesozoic basin.

24

convective flow of heat within the earth, are now believed to be responsible for both the collision of continents and their eventual separation. Geologists refer to these processes collectively as Plate Tectonics.

Gradually, the Atlantic Ocean filled the widening abyss between the separating continents. As they moved slowly apart, the plates with their continents realigned themselves geographically (Figure 9). North America rotated counterclockwise from an equatorial position to a north to south orientation, and South America, Antarctica and Australia all broke away from Africa. The rocks that were deposited on the margin of the North American plate in equatorial seas over two hundred fifty million years ago during the Paleozoic Era were carried toward the north polar region. This juxtaposition of tropical coal beds and coral reefs with a modern polar desert seemed incongruous to geologists of the early twentieth century. It was not until the 1960's that plate tectonics as a working geological hypothesis unlocked these mysteries.

As the ocean basin widened and the continents moved apart, the sea flooded the continental lowlands, and sediments eroded from the continents were piled layer

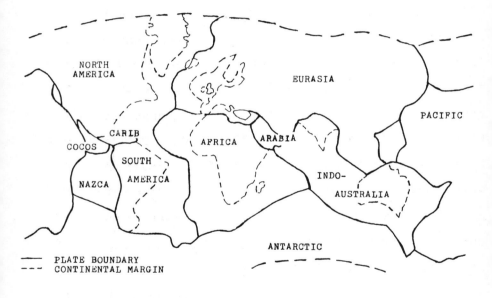

Figure 9. A generalized map of crustal plates.

upon layer on the new shallow sea bed. Between the Jurassic Period and the present, sediment layers accumulated to form a wedge of coastal plain and continental shelf sediments thousands of feet thick. The shelf south of the present Rhode Island coast includes nearly one thousand feet of Upper Cretaceous deposits beneath Block Island (Figure 3b).

During the Tertiary Period between sixty five and two million years ago, layers of marine sediment were deposited well to the east of the Block Island. Glacially thrusted beds of Tertiary marine strata that contain fish and marine mammal fossils crop out in the terminal moraine in Martha's Vineyard. Tertiary beds were not deposited in the Block Island shelf sequences which were above sea level at that time. The Island does have late Cretaceous sands and clays that contain thin seams of lignite, a soft coal-like material, and nodules of iron pyrite, called fool's gold, that formed in ancient wetlands on the oceanic margin of a Cretaceous delta. Unfortunately for fossil collectors, no dinosaurs have been found among the carbonized plant impressions in the Cretaceous strata. Like the Tertiary strata of Martha's Vineyard, the Cretaceous beds in the moraines of

Block Island at Clay Head and on the southeast coast are not in their original position. They were transported by the glacier several miles south of their sea-floor outcroppings to Block Island. They now reside as disoriented masses of sediment stuck in the moraines along with rock debris from Paleozoic rock formations of the mainland.

The boulders on the beach are examples of erratics, samples of Paleozoic bedrock that are out of context in their present location. These rocks are a reminder of Paleozoic plate tectonics and contain minerals that reveal their origins deep in the crust. The Paleozoic rocks are the result of the collisions between oceanic and continental plates and the intrusion of igneous rocks and rifting of the crust. With these clues in hand, we can envision the collisions and separations of plates, as well as volcanic island arcs standing off the coast of the ancient continent. Granite boulders suggest ancient batholiths, while the green and black cobbles on the beach may be derived from the oceanic crust or subcrustal realms. Erosion of thousands of feet of bedrock since Paleozoic time has exposed the mainland rocks to the work of the glaciers that in turn brought the rock fragments to create the moraines. Conveniently, rocks from differing northern terranes help identify the source, or provenance, of the glacial deposits of the Island.

GLACIATIONS

In the sixty-three million year interval of the Tertiary Period, the Cretaceous strata of the coastal plain stood above sea level. The shoreline was tens of miles south and east of Block Island, and rivers from the mountains dissected the plain and excavated deep valleys. The upland of the coastal plain was comprised of the hills between the river valleys. The southern New England coast, as we know it, from eastern Long Island to Cape Cod, was nowhere to be seen in this ancient geography. We can only infer from the shape of the sea floor what the land might have looked like before the last glacier arrived (Figure 3a and 5).

It is probable when glaciations began early in the Pleistocene Epoch, the advancing ice flowed like a river filling the lowlands, thinning over the hills, and extending out of the major valleys as lobes of debris-laden ice. In the nineteenth century, many geologists believed there had been four Pleistocene glaciations in North America. The sediments of each of the glaciations and the intervening warm intervals, the interglacials, were assumed to have been universally deposited like the layers of a cake. Today we know there were more than sixteen glaciations during a few major glacial stages. The deposits of most glaciations were limited in geographic extent. Few glaciers reached the maximum glacial limit, and erosion has removed much of the sediment.

In southern New England, including Block Island, there is evidence of only two glaciations. The most recent of these reached its greatest extent twenty-two thousand years ago late in the Pleistocene Epoch (Figure 10). This glacier, the Laurentide Ice Sheet, advanced in the latter part of the Wisconsinan Stage. The earlier glaciation took place either before forty thousand years ago in the early part of the Wisconsinan Stage, or more than one hundred forty thousand years ago in the next older glacial stage, the Illinoian.

The shape of the land influenced the flow of the ice during both glaciations. Major land forms, like the Narragansett Bay lowland and the Rhode Island-Connecticut upland, gave the ice a directional flow fabric, orienting the rock fragments in the ice in the direction of ice movement and shaping the ice front into lobes. Field

PERIOD	EPOCHS	STAGES	AGE yrs	EVENTS
Quaternary	Holocene	Recent	0-10,000	N and S BI joined, sea level rise
		Late	10,000-	Sea Level Rise; Glacial lakes drain 12,000.
			20,000	BI ice free. Glacier retreats.
	Pleistocene	Wisconsinan	22,000	Glaciation; low sea level
		Mid-Wisconsinan	30,000	Warm Interval Sea level rises
		Early Wisconsinan	60,000	Glaciation; low sea level
		Sangamon	125,000	Interglacial; High sea level
		Illinoian	140,000-200,000	Early (first) BI glaciation (?)
		Early Stages	200,000-2,000,000	Interglacials & Glacials

Figure 10. Quaternary Period Time Scale, 0 to 2 my

studies of glacial deposits in southern New England, particularly Block Island, show the existence of two distinct layers of glacial deposits, known as drift sheets. These were the products of the two glaciations; the lower, or older, drift sheet was the first to arrive. It derived from a glacial lobe that traversed the Narragansett Bay area from the northeast. The upper, or younger, drift sheet was deposited from a lobe of the second glacier; this one crossed western Rhode Island and eastern Connecticut from the northwest.

THE LOWER, OLDER DRIFT

The older of the two drifts predates the limit of radiocarbon dating, which is about forty thousand years. In order to establish a finite age for this glacial sediment, another radioactive element, like uranium, must be found. Uranium occurs in igneous rocks as well as the shells of marine animals that extract this element from sea water. Since no late Pleistocene igneous rocks were formed at the same time as this drift, marine shells could supply a clue to the age.

If the interval between the first and second glaciations was significantly warm, and sea level rose high enough, warm-water marine animals could have lived in the sea north of Block Island. Coral, a mainly tropical animal, fixes uranium from sea water in the crystals of its shells and is a good source for uranium-series dating. The presence of coral, even if it was picked up by the last glacier and redeposited in the moraine, would confirm the age and occurrence of a warm interval and provide a minimum age for the first glaciation. In Nantucket, a fragment of coral that had been redeposited in a marine sand layer in the Sankaty Cliffs was dated at about one hundred twenty-eight thousand years old. While not a finite age for the sand unit, the coral and the date reveal an interglacial episode.

The geological record of this part of the Atlantic coastal plain shows it was affected by at least two warm intervals in the late Pleistocene. The older, the Sangamon Interglacial, peaked around one hundred twenty-five thousand years ago (Figure 10). It separates the Illinoian and Wisconsinan glacial stages, and it was warmer than and had a sea level about ten feet higher than exists today. The younger warm episode, a mid-Wisconsinan interstadial, was centered around thirty thousand years ago, but it was not as warm as the Sangamon, and the sea was about sixty feet shy of its modern level.

In Long Island, the mid-Wisconsinan interstadial is dated between thirty thousand and twenty-eight thousand years ago in both undisturbed marine strata off the south shore, and in glacially-transported marine sediments. Reefs of oyster shells, salt marsh peat and clay were excavated from the floor of a marine embayment north of Long Island and then redeposited in the terminal moraine by the last ice sheet. These sediments, known as the Portwashingtonian beds after their location on Long Island, belong to a sequence of marine and glacial deposits radiocarbon dated between greater than forty thousand years and twenty-two thousand years ago. Wood found in glacial till interbedded with this organic sequence dates the arrival of the Laurentide glacier on Long Island as twenty-two thousand years ago. The interstadial Portwashingtonian beds, located between the drift sheets of the older and younger glaciations, establish the minimum age of forty thousand years for the older deposits. Through their fossil content, mainly the oysters and pollen of evergreen and hardwood trees, these beds also provide us with a glimpse of cold and temperate climates and spruce, pine and oak forests during that interval.

By extrapolating the Portwashingtonian and Sankaty ages to Block Island, where theoretically there are matching sediments, we can infer that the older drift sheet was deposited before forty thousand years ago, either in early Wisconsinan time, perhaps sixty thousand years ago, or during the Illinoian glaciation, more than one hundred forty thousand years ago. The younger age would be in keeping with the sequence of ages and climatic conditions in the Long Island record. Fossil spruce pollen indicate cold climatic conditions around forty thousand years ago and may indicate a warming trend following an earlier glaciation.

Support for an Illinoian age for the earlier glaciation is based on the distribution of glacial deposits and the inferred geographic extent of the two ice sheets. Some geologists limit the early Wisconsinan glacier to the Lake Ontario and St. Lawrence Valley region. This makes an Illinoian age for the early glaciation worth considering. We can also note that the flow fabric and rock types in the older drift indicate expansion of the ice southward across the Narragansett Bay lowland, covering Block Island and extending as far westward as the Montauk Peninsula of Long Island. At Montauk a thirty-eight thousand year age has been determined for organic sediment found between the drift sheets. These deposits are equivalent to the older and younger drift sheets of Block Island.

The older drift forms the bulwark of the bluffs of both Montauk Point and Block Island, where it is seen most dramatically in exposures between Mohegan Bluffs and Dickens Point. It often appears to be dark gray in color, crudely stratified and with lenses of sand and beds of lake clay and silt. This drift is also deformed, contorted into tight folds, ripped into large blocks and thrusted southward. Many of the ripped-up blocks are surrounded by the light-colored sands of the upper drift. This dramatic damage seems to have been done during the southward advance of the younger glacier which filled in behind the folds and thrusts with sand and gravel washed out of the melting ice.

The older drift also contains compact basal till, an unsorted and unstratified glacial sediment that was deposited directly beneath the ice sheet. In an undisturbed condition, this till is relatively impermeable and resists infiltration by surface water. While the till has a low proportion of clay, its compaction allows groundwater to pond on its surface and infiltrate slowly. This drift sheet as a whole is continuous beneath the surface layer of younger drift; the ripped-up blocks of till are seen in the bluffs as local features.

At the height of the first glaciation, the ice over Block Island could have been a few hundred feet thick, tapering to a terminus several miles to the south. As the glacier receded, a lake formed between the ice margin and the terminal moraine, and layers of clay and silt accumulated on the lake floor. Forward movement of the ice and collapse of the sediments due to melting deformed the lake beds and drained the lake. Later, these beds were crumpled into tight folds by the last glacier. At the end of the early glaciation, the place where Block Island would eventually take shape was buried somewhere in the middle of the terminal moraine of that glacier.

THE UPPER, YOUNGER DRIFT

The upper drift sheet, the layer of sediments deposited by the late Wisconsinan glacier, overlies the lower, older, drift sheet and covers much of the Island. The younger drift is characterized by glacial deposits and landforms that are associated with a melting and receding glacier. It is made up, in part, of a type of till, known as meltout till, deposited during melting of the ice. The meltout till often overlies water-laid sediment, or outwash, which is both stratified and sorted in grain size by running water. Where meltwater flows from the ice to the adjacent ground surface, the outwash piles up into conical hills called kames. When meltwater flows directly from the ice into standing water, the outwash forms kame deltas. Lakes are common features of a decaying ice front between the glacier and the moraines. Lake deltas are built where streams flow overland into a lake. Sand and gravel collect to form the upper beds of the delta, the topset beds, at water level, and fine sediment filters down onto the lake floor and collects in layers of silt and clay, known as the bottomset beds. More steeply pitched sand layers between the topsets and the bottomsets are the foreset beds. A broad expanse of outwash in front of the moraine is an outwash plain. Long Island and Martha's Vineyard each have an extensive outwash plain onshore; Block Island's outwash plain may be several miles to the south, but like the moraine, it is beneath the sea.

The upper drift sheet contrasts in sedimentary and structural characteristics with the lower drift sheet. The physical deformation of the lower drift by the last ice is impressive. Light-colored sands of the upper drift engulf ripped-up blocks of lower drift. The sands also overlie the deformed lower drift and have been folded by the overriding ice. Lower drift and upper outwash deposits are usually covered by meltout till, evidence of ice melting nearby. When we view the bluffs of Block Island, we are looking at a portion of the moraine well north of the glacial terminus. Both the first and the last ice sheets extended south of the bluffs, and considerable glacial sediment has been removed by rising sea level and coastal erosion over the last twelve thousand years. On the east side of the Island, we can see the remnants of the moraines of both the older and younger glaciations, exposed in the bluffs in a cross section from south to north.

At Mohegan Bluffs, there are over one hundred forty feet of both the lower and upper drift sheets etched out in relief. At first it is hard to distinguish the deformed and reorganized lower drift from the undeformed and, in place, lower drift below it. However, the light-colored outwash of the upper drift contrasts with and surrounds the ice-shoved, darker lower drift. They differ in color because of their source materials, and the fabric and rock types in the upper drift point to a northwesterly source. This drift is rich in pebbles from the granitic and gneissic bedrock in southern Rhode Island and eastern Connecticut over which the last glacier advanced. The ice picked up rock debris ranging in size from erratic boulders to gravel and sand and covered the Island with this material.

While this glacier deposited sediment well beyond the southerly bluffs, the crest of its most prominent ice margin on southern Block Island runs east-west through Beacon Hill. Here the ice remained long enough to build a recessional moraine, the Beacon Hill Moraine, out of meltout till and outwash. Today, the surface of the Island still looks much like it probably did after of the last glacier melted.

When the glacier still covered the Island north of the Beacon Hill Moraine , meltwater streaming from the ice cut deep, south-trending valleys into the drift. Prominent among these meltwater channels are Rodman Hollow and the Fresh Pond-Peckham Pond-Mitchell Pond lineation. As a glacial stream bed, Rodman Hollow originally sloped southward from the Beacon Hill Moraine, now at an elevation of one hundred fifty feet, over seventy miles downslope to its junction with the late Wisconsinan sea near the edge of the continental shelf, with a drop in elevation of almost five hundred feet. The topography shows that the Rodman Hollow meltwater channel also has three depressions deepened below this gradient. The most southerly of these is only about thirty feet above present sea level.

These depressions, known as kettles, indicate that large blocks of ice were embedded in the drift as the ice front receded to the Beacon Hill position. Meltwater escaped southward in the Rodman Hollow meltwater channel over this ice-cored outwash. As the buried ice melted, the kettles formed, and the valley took on its irregular shape. However, rather than three ponds occupying the kettle holes, the channel has remained dry. It is probable the ice cut through the relatively impermeable till of the lower drift allowing meltwater to drain into porous sediments below. Today rain water falling in the channel quickly infiltrates these sediments.

By contrast, the Fresh Pond- Peckham Pond- Mitchell Pond meltwater channel, appearing as a string of kettles with ponds, does support a water table. Apparently, the ice did not penetrate the lower till, and the channel was plugged to the south by glacial sediment. Melting of the ice created the kettles, and groundwater accumulated on the till to form ponds. Chains of ponds in meltwater valleys, like the Fresh Pond group, have been likened to rosary beads and are known as paternoster (our father) lakes.

The southern bluffs of Block Island also reveal both the power of the ice to deform and the ability of meltwater to dissect layers of sediment. By looking at the materials in front of us, we can appreciate the energy involved in the deposition of outwash, channel gravels, lake beds, and the variety of drift that makes up a moraine and its landforms.

As the ice sheet melted and the ice front receded, large quantities of sediment and water were released.

Meltwater ponded south of the moraine and cascaded along channels. Buried blocks of ice melted to form kettles. Some kettles in the headwaters of meltwater channels quickly filled with glacial silt; today the relict lake beds appear as flat fields, like the meadows of The Plains and the headwaters of Rodman Hollow on the distal (south) slope of the Beacon Hill Moraine.

In a special circumstance of erosion, lake beds-normally a depressed feature- can be raised above the surrounding landscape as inverted topography. Inverted topography is the result of erosion around a low landform like a lake bed or stream channel. With removal of the surrounding sediment, this feature becomes elevated above the adjacent land. A good example of this is in Indian Head Neck which extends as an elliptical ridge southwestward into Great Salt Pond.

Geologically, Indian Head Neck is carved from a deposit of proglacial lake sediments made up of over one hundred thin-bedded sets of light and dark-colored layers of silt, sand and clay. These beds can be seen from Great Salt Pond, but the scale of the bedding can only be appreciated on close inspection. The pairs of beds, which are called varves, consist of dark-colored silt and clay that alternate with light-colored, fine grained sand. They are believed to represent the accumulation of sediment on the lake floor over the course of one year. The fine sand layers form during spring and summer when the sediment is coarser due to increased water flow and oxidized through exposure to the atmosphere. The clay-silt layers are from very fine sediment suspended in the water when the lake is frozen over. The unoxidized fine particles settle out of the winter-stilled lake to form the thin, dark layer.

The one hundred varves in the Indian Head Neck lake would represent a one hundred year record of deposition in a glacial lake that formed between the glacier and the moraine to the south during recession of the ice front. The position of the lake bed may have been predetermined by the Great Salt Pond trough, which is aligned roughly north northwest to south southeast. This confirms the direction of advance of the last ice sheet as determined from provenance and fabric studies.

A further complication in the geology of glacial recession occurs when a short-term, cold climate interval causes the ice to pause in its recession and even to readvance. Prior to the late-Wisconsinan readvance the ice stood north of the Great Salt Pond trough. The renewed energy of the readvancing ice carved existing drift into elliptical hills called drumlins. These egg-shaped hills have steep slopes facing the ice and smooth slopes downstream. The Indian Head Neck lake beds were in the path of the readvancing glacier; the result was this drumlin-shaped ridge. This ice also carved other low hills of the moraine into drumlin shapes before it came to rest against the north, or proximal, slope of the Beacon Hill Moraine. A cluster of drumlins borders Great Salt Pond and Harbor Pond; along with Indian Head Neck, these hills create the picturesque landscape between New Harbor and Old Harbor.

Many of the other lakes of the Island occupy kettles. For these lakes, the ice must have rested on impermeable sediment like the till of the lower drift. As water filled the kettle, fine sediment carried into the basin by surface runoff helped to seal off its bottom layer. Ultimately, kettle lakes can fill up with layers of sediment and may be transformed into peat bogs as aquatic vegetation grows across the shallows.

While coastal erosion may have removed the most southerly deposits of the last glacier, the Beacon Hill

Moraine and the recessional topography to the north are clear reminders of that ice age. The recessional moraine that forms the northern lobe of the Island is known as the Corn Neck Moraine (Figure 4). With its highlands of Bush Lot Hill and Clay Head, its hummocky topography is also dotted with kettles. The upper drift covers till of the lower drift and occasional masses of Cretaceous sediment. The bluffs along the northeast coast reveal deformation of the drift sheets and the mobilization of Cretaceous clays that are leached out of the sediments by groundwater. A sandy delta, nearly forty feet thick stands high in the northeasterly cliffs marking the location of a proglacial lake that formed as the ice front retreated to that position. A veneer of meltout till caps the glacial sequence and represents the last deposits of the wasting ice on Block Island. After the ice receded, this till was covered by wind-blown silts called loess. More recently sand dunes have formed on the Island's bluffs.

POSTGLACIAL SEDIMENTS, CHRONOLOGY, AND VEGETATION

The chronology of late Pleistocene events depends on a time scale based on the radiocarbon dating of organic sediments found both in Block Island and Long Island. At Port Washington, Long Island, glacial till containing spruce wood is dated at twenty-two thousand years, establishing the time of arrival of the late Wisconsinan glacier on Long Island and the deposition of the terminal moraine. Assuming the Connecticut-Rhode Island Lobe of the late Wisconsinan glacier which formed Block Island was synchronous with the Hudson Lobe that reached Port Washington in western Long Island, then the terminal moraine south of Block Island was deposited at the same time. We can also assume younger ages- perhaps as much as one thousand years- for the Beacon Hill Recessional Moraine and the Corn Neck Recessional Moraine on Block Island.

Recession of the ice from the terminal position and across the future site of Block Island probably took two thousand years, so that the Island was ice free around twenty thousand years ago. This chronology is confirmed by a radiocarbon date showing that nineteen thousand years ago the Hudson Lobe of the Wisconsinan glacier had receded to the latitude of White Plains, New York, well north of the terminal moraine. With this timetable, it is apparent that the last ice sheet did its work, left its deposits, and departed in relatively quick order.

After the glacier retreated from Block Island, it paused to form a major recessional moraine to the north. This moraine is seen in the west to east trend of hills and islands that link up the Roanoake Point Moraine of the northeast coast of Long Island with the Fishers Island Moraine south of the Connecticut coast, and then eastward to the Charlestown Moraine and Point Judith Moraine in southern Rhode Island (Figure 4).

To understand what happened on Block Island after the ice left twenty thousand years ago, we must examine some established relationships. As continental glaciers advanced, cooler climate forced vegetation to migrate southward into more favorable regions. It is not that plants can pick up their roots and run for it, but successive generations propogate where soil and climate are more suitable. In eastern North America, the forests and ground-cover vegetation had already achieved both a latitudinal and an altitudinal stratification over millions of years of climatic changes.

Vegetational shifts occurred before and after the mid-Wisconsinan warm interval thirty thousand years ago. Oak forests, indicators of temperate climate, succeeded the earlier spruce forests generally associated with cooler conditions. The oaks were later replaced by forests of spruce and pine, suggesting a renewed cooler climate. During full glaciation around twenty-two thousand years ago, oak hardwood forests had migrated southward to southern Florida. Spruce and pine followed the cool climate, ranging into northern Florida, and a swath of Arctic tundra filled in between the ice front and the coniferous forest. In some areas, climatic refuges enabled plant and animal species to survive the ice age. So while Block Island-to-be was under the ice, twenty-two thousand years ago, lands to the south, including the present continental shelf, were above sea level and vegetated by plants of varying resistance to the cold (Figure 3a).

During warmer climatic intervals between glaciations, like the Sangamon Interglacial, the mid-Wisconsinan interstadial, and the present postglacial episode, sea level rose as glaciers melted and vegetation migrated northward. Near the ice front arctic shrubs like birch, alder, willow, and tundra herbs migrating along with the ice front, pioneered on fresh deposits of outwash, and spruce thrived on rocky glacial soils and in wetlands. Later, pines became established on well-drained sandy soils. Forests of oak and hickory with other temperate species followed the pines into southern New England, inheriting the loamy glaciated terrain.

The postglacial record for the Island began shortly after the ice receded twenty thousand years ago, at a time when the climate was still rigorous. Winds crossing the barren land surface adjacent to the ice swept silt out of the glacial deposits and laid a blanket of finely ground rock, known as loess, over the moraines. Up to three feet of loess can be found in places on Block Island. At the same time, the daily freeze and thaw of the wet soils enabled them to flow over the frozen glacial deposits below. Excavations for new home sites reveal solifluction (soil flow) bands and contorted layers formed by this process.

Vegetation invaded this barren, deglaciated landscape, and the plants shed their pollen and spores into the layers of sediments on the floors of ponds and bogs. This accumulation of plant debris has provided the text of the Island's vegetational history. This story has been reconstructed from fossil pollen found in sediment cores taken from bogs and kettle lakes. Each layer of sediment, from the glacial deposits at the bottom of the depression to the peat at its surface, yields an assemblage of pollen representing plants growing in the area at the time of deposition. Layer by layer the pollen spectra reveal differences in climate and vegetation. The accompanying diagram summarizes the pollen data from three Island sites: Great Swamp, a bog on Corn Neck, and the varves at Indian Head Neck (Figure 11). Read horizontally, the percentages of pollen types indicate the relative abundance of each plant at that level or time; the variety of plants suggests the overall vegetation. The vertical profiles show the relative abundance of each plant type over time.

The pollen record documents the migration of the vegetation northward as the ice receded. The oldest of the postglacial pollen-bearing deposits are the Indian Head Neck varves and the deepest bog sediments from Great Swamp. They both contain tundra shrubs and herbs, including pine, birch, willow, alder, mountain avens,

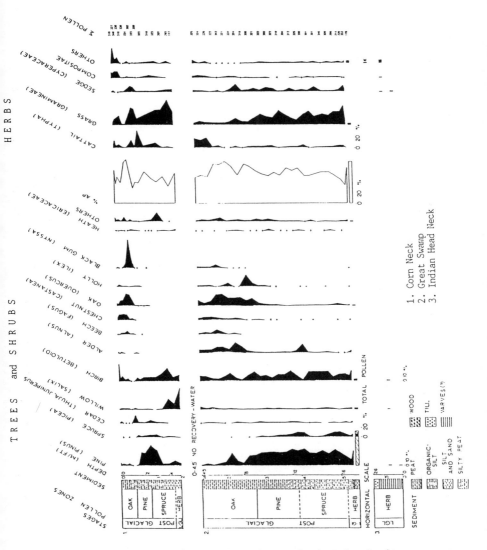

Figure 11a. Pollen diagram for three Block Island sites.

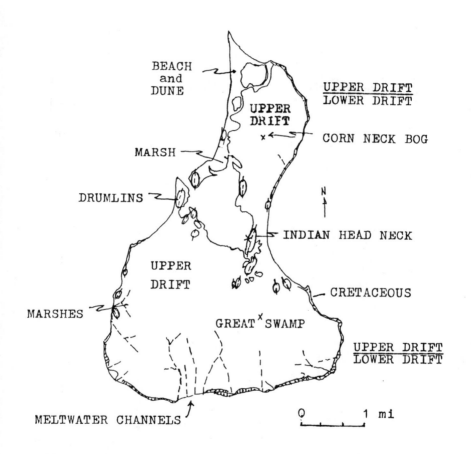

BEACH
and
DUNE

UPPER DRIFT
LOWER DRIFT

UPPER
DRIFT

CORN NECK BOG

MARSH

DRUMLINS

N

UPPER
DRIFT

INDIAN HEAD NECK

MARSHES

CRETACEOUS

GREAT SWAMP

UPPER DRIFT
LOWER DRIFT

MELTWATER CHANNELS

0   1 mi

Figure 11b. A generalized geologic map of Block Island.

54

Figure 11c. The glacial varves at Indian Head Neck.

Figure 11d. Detail of the Indian Head Neck varves depicting an ice-contact feature: an ice-rafted stone in a high angle fault, collapse zone.

Figure 11e.   The geology of Mohegan Bluffs. Note the deeply gullied lower drift below and the bouldery meltout upper drift in the top layer.

grass and sedge. These plants confirm the presence of tundra even as the ice receded. Pollen assemblages from these deposits are collectively referred to the Herb Pollen Zone. In succeeding layers of sediment, pollen assemblages are dominated by spruce and record the northward advance of spruce forests. This interval is designated the Spruce Pollen Zone. The prominance of spruce forests can be traced from around nineteen thousand years to about eleven thousand years ago, about the same time that people were finding their way from Siberia to North America across the Bering Land Bridge. Similar communities of plants and plant successions, including tundra and spruce forests, are found in southern Alaska where glaciers are receding today.

The next forests are represented in the bog sediments by an abundance of pine pollen, first in association with birch and grass and later with oak. Pine forest succeeded spruce in the northward migrations and prevailed until around eight thousand years ago. Although the Pine Pollen Zone is of shorter duration, its signature is consistent in all of the pollen records in this region where somewhat warmer and drier climate proved favorable to pine. Pine forests migrated northward selecting well-drained sandy tracts of outwash, lake beds and river terraces, while spruce moved further north and higher into the mountains.

The onset of cool and wet conditions around nine thousand years ago enabled hardwood forests to overtake the conifers. The Oak Pollen Zone in the upper part of the record begins with an abundance of oak and pine, then a variety of trees including holly, cedar, alder, birch, willow, beech, chestnut, and black gum enter the record.

At the time of European colonization, the Island supported a complex hardwood forest. This forest was rapidly depleted during land clearing for farming and burning of wood for fuel, and by the middle of the eighteenth century, it was largely consumed. Colonial land clearing is indicated in the pollen record in the abrupt increase in composites, a feature that is quite apparent in the Corn Neck bog pollen diagram. Composites, a large group of common herbs, including aster, ragweed, ragged sailor, and goldenrod, invade open or disturbed ground. This marker is missing at Great Swamp where the pollen record is truncated, presumably because the upper layers of peat were dug for fuel to replace wood. Not only had the trees been cut, but so had the peat in the relentless conversion of Block Island from forest to farmland. A Department of Energy survey of peat resources of the Island in the late 1980's showed that peat was still abundant in most localities. Many bogs like the Corn Neck bog had not been mined, and in large wetlands the peat is quite thick; some parts of Great Swamp still have over ten feet of peat below the surface. It is our good fortune that bogs have preserved the vegetational and climatic record of the Island's postglacial interval.

At the same time that the vegetation was changing, the land-sea boundaries of Block Island and the surrounding region were being profoundly altered. The sea gradually covered the continental shelf, and the higher hills of the moraines became islands, exposed to the ravages of time and geologic processes. Between twenty thousand and twelve thousand years ago sea level rose over two hundred feet. About twelve thousand years ago the terminal moraine was breached, and the glacial lakes in Long Island Sound drained into the ocean. Block Island was a much larger island, shaped by the rivers that cut through the moraines (Figure 5). Submerged tracts of the moraines are reminders of their former extensions between the islands (Figure 4). The sea continued to rise for the next six thousand years, nearly reaching its modern level. At that time, Block Island was cut into two islands. These segments were slowly joined by barrier beaches as the sea continued to rise at an average rate of one foot per century. But the Island was eroded in the process, as it supplied the sand for the barriers. The geologic future of Block Island will depend on the rate of sea level rise over the next few centuries. Theoretically, the sea could once again cut the Island in two (Figure 5).

GEOLOGIC PROCESSES

Since the melting of the last glacier, the ice-free
surface of the terminal moraine region has been exposed
to the atmosphere. As a segment of the moraine, Block
Island represents both glacial and coastal terrain that
has stood against the weather for over twenty thousand
years. Keep in mind that after deglaciation the rising
sea did not reach the moraine for nearly eight thousand
years. Block Island was part of a long ridge with a few
high hills that became the offshore islands of today. The
region looked more like the straight coast of New Jersey
than the jagged coast of southern New England.

SOILS

With the melting of the ice, the glacial deposits
were exposed to the dynamics of the atmosphere. Over the
course of thousands of years, the minerals in the ground-
up rock debris slowly decayed and disintegrated to form
layers of soil along with an assortment of compounds

capable of supporting plant and animal life. Rock-forming minerals like feldspar and mica, rich in potassium and aluminum, were converted into clays. Carbon compounds and water were released to the soil, and iron and aluminum combined with oxygen to form oxides. Rain water percolated into the soil from above and dissolved some solids and redeposited them in the deeper sediments. Organic debris from plants, added at the surface along with the by-products of decay, enriched the soil and provided carbonates and humic acid to the mix.

Typically, soils in humid regions like southern New England develop three distinct soil horizons or zones (Figure 12). The lowest, designated the C soil zone , is most like the original or parent material: bedrock or transported rock debris, like the glacial deposits of Block Island, which range in particle size from clay to boulders.

Above the C zone is the B soil zone, which consists of sediments that have been considerably altered from their C zone source. They often have a higher water content, due partly to the water table that collects on glacial till. Soil water seeps through the B zone carrying many compounds of clay, iron and aluminum

Soil   Infiltration   Characteristics
Zones

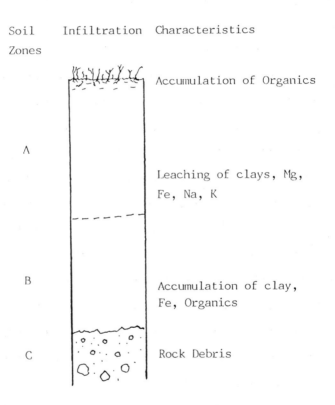

Accumulation of Organics

A

Leaching of clays, Mg,
Fe, Na, K

B

Accumulation of clay,
Fe, Organics

C

Rock Debris

Figure 12. A generalized soil profile.

oxides, carbonates and humus. These materials are deposited lower down in the B zone, also known as the zone of accumulation. They form mineral horizons, like the red-colored, iron oxide-cemented bands that are typical of this soil zone.

The uppermost zone, the A soil zone, includes an organic-rich layer with abundant roots and organic litter at the surface, and typically a white, leached horizon that supplied oxides to the B zone; thus the name, zone of leaching, for the A zone. Plants supply the organic compounds, and rainwater mixing with humus and carbonates forms weak acids that help dissolve A zone minerals and transport them to the B zone; in the last century, rainwater has become somewhat acidic, due to sulfuric aerosols from the burning of fossil fuels.

Soils formed on glacial drift are commonly called loam, a mixture of sand, silt and clay, and clay loam or sandy loam, depending on the dominant grain size. Block Island loams have traditionally been given mainland geographic names, like Narragansett sandy loam and Gloucester sandy loam, the latter being the stony variety derived from glacial till. The thick loess cover on the Island gives rise to a silty variety of loam that makes a good agricultural soil because of the fine-grained, unaltered mineral particles. The sand in the sandy loams is derived mainly from quartz-rich granite and gneiss gravels. Quartz is a mineral that weathers very slowly, changing size as opposed to decomposing.

Technically, these soils are Pedalfers, those rich in aluminum and iron, and are characteristic of humid and temperate climate. The pedalfers of southern New England are also called gray-brown podzolic soils, and in a more recent classification, spodosols. These soils normally are initiated in a cool climate in a forested region with abundant organic materials, like that of early, postglacial Block Island. It is hard to imagine the Island covered with a hardwood forest, but it existed that way prior to the clear cutting of the trees in colonial time. Both the postglacial loess and the glacial drift, now covered by loess and sand dunes, may have old soil profiles, called paleosols, which are significant indicators of past soil-forming environments.

The organic soils of peat bogs are quite different in composition, because they are rich in partially decomposed plant debris but have little mineral content. Pollen, spores, seeds, needles, and other tough plant structures are preserved in the layers of peat. Many glacial lakes have been filled in with lake bottom sediment and then covered with peat. These layers of sediment have provided the record of postglacial vegetation and climate in their assemblages of tree, shrub, and herb pollen. As discussed earlier, this important aspect of Island history can only be found in the sediments of local bogs.

While lakes support aquatic vegetation, increased nutrients, including terrestrial pollutants, in the water can generate blooms, or population explosions, of algae and grasses that can threaten a lake's existence. Left uncorrected, this process leads to early filling of the lake with organic debris, which has happened to many kettle lakes on Block Island.

Sand dunes and beach deposits normally have very little soil development and very weak soil zones. These soils, known as entisols, may support vegetation like dune grass and beach rose. Soil zone development on these sediments can be interrupted by coastal erosion associated with major storms.

WEATHERING

Rock fragments begin to break down after prolonged exposure to changing atmospheric conditions. Weathering involves both chemical decomposition of mineral compounds and physical disintegration of mineral grains. Both processes are augmented by the presence of water, which acts as a solvent in chemical reactions removing bonding minerals, and as a mechanical wedge separating mineral grains and opening up planes of weakness in rocks. This activity is accelerated when water freezes and expands to form ice.

Rainfall combines with certain elements and compounds to form acids and bases which can weaken chemical bonds and release water and gases. Some minerals are turned to clay; others become grains of sand. Feldspars, micas and iron and magnesium-rich minerals break down rapidly, while quartz is very resistant and makes up most of the sand at the beach. Oxygen combines with iron and aluminum to form oxides which are carried by water to favorable environments of deposition. Water will also be incorporated in the hydrous forms of some minerals.

Physically, water seeps into partings in rocks and

pore spaces between mineral grains where it can freeze, expand and wedge the rock or mineral grains apart. It can saturate a thin rind of rock that will eventually peel away in a spherical layer, like the skin of an orange. We can find erratics on the beach that exhibit weathering rinds, and some have split from repeated freeze and thaw. The more massive crystalline rocks seem to disintegrate readily; finer-grained metamorphic rocks, like schist, more often decompose completely. It is not uncommon to find thoroughly rotted boulders of schist buried in water-saturated drift.

The rate at which weathering processes proceed varies considerably and is enhanced by water seepage. We can get an idea of short-term weathering in a humid climate from headstones of various rock types in the cemetery. A dated headstone reveals how long that rock has been exposed, and its condition shows the relative amount of weathering. We can only estimate the rate of development of rinds, the loosening of mineral grains and the separation of metamorphic foliations and bedding planes. Slate headstones can weather rapidly if the slaty partings absorb water. These may lose layers along with the inscriptions in only a few generations. Rocks like granite with large crystals are affected by freeze and thaw which separates the mineral grains. Polishing protects the decorative rock faces from acidation and water seepage. Red sandstone markers are apt to disintegrate in only a few decades and are rarely used in modern cemeteries, even though tightly compressed and cemented sandstones and flagstones will resist both frost wedging and corrosion. Serpentine-rich headstones are susceptible to air pollution, mainly acid rain, and are less widely used.

MASS WASTING

Mass wasting involves the movement of rock materials downslope in response to gravity aided by water content. It ranges in magnitude and rate of movement from the nearly imperceptible soil creep on gentle slopes to the abrupt fall of sedimentary debris from cliffs and the wholesale slumping and sliding of massive blocks of moraine along sea cliffs. Movement can be of sufficient size to damage and dislodge surface features, including buildings, whether cottages or lighthouses, perched at the edge of a sea cliff.

Debris falls build cone-shaped piles of sediment at the base of cliffs, and single boulders tumble down to the beach. Large erratics lodged in the moraine are the local equivalent of a falling rock zone as they sit precariously overhead with little to hold them back. Downslope movement of sediment can be initiated by water saturation that turns soft, fine-grained materials into mud flows. Saturated clay beds become "quick clays" when flow is triggered by a short-term disturbance, from a footfall to an earthquake.

Slumping is the result of a number of factors, including rainwater infiltration, saturation of clays, erosion of the cliff face, wave erosion at the base, and the orientation of the layers of sediment or rock. It is a prominent characteristic of the Island's bluffs. Coarse, compacted sediment like glacial till, can slide rapidly on a water-lubricated clay layer. Along the eastern coast of the Island, masses of clay-rich Cretaceous sediments facilitate slumping of large blocks of drift.

Slumps begin when ground water seeps into porous soil and moves downward along planes of weakness. These planes form around dislocated blocks of lower drift and along surfaces of impermeable sediment. They gradually evolve into faults that extend downward from the seepage zone to the base of the slope as rotational planes (Figure 13). A sign of a new fracture forming along the surface may be a line of green grass or more robust shrubs because water collects in the opening. As the slump progresses a small offset or sag, like a miniature cliff, may appear. When the space between the slump block and the solid land becomes large enough, water will accumulate to form a sag pond. Water entering the rotational plane continues to lubricate the fault zone and encourage slipping. Irregularly-shaped, sliding blocks of lower till are gradually etched out by rainwater erosion and whittled into deep gullies, monuments and pinnacles to form a jumbled badland of odd-shaped remnants, known as hoodoos, between the bluff and the beach. Old slumps can be recognized because their block-shaped remnants stand out from the wall of the bluff. The step-like tops of the slumped blocks are still covered with growing vegetation, but they are lower than the original surface and are tilted back toward the land. These outliers are actually slowly rotating slumps

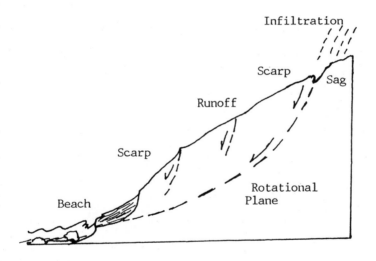

Figure 13a. Profile of a sea cliff slump block.

Figure 13b.   Slumps in the bluffs and a sand slide forming a cone at the base.

detached from the bluff and sliding along the curved fault line. With on-going wave erosion at the base of the bluff, the block migrates downward toward the beach where it gradually erodes.

As more water is added to this system, rapid movement can be triggered. If fine-grained sediments make up some of the layers, flows may accompany the slump. While slumps, slides and flows are common types of slope failure on coastal bluffs, they seem to develop without warning. Even though the slumping process is slow, with all of the characteristics of mass wasting present, slopes are in a continual state of adjustment. It is important to know that natural processes are accelerated by construction projects that disrupt the sediment layers, such as digging cellar holes, laying water and drainage pipe and installing septic systems, which also add water to the ground. Any activity that reorganizes sediment layers will enable water to infiltrate the surface. Any channel dug into the sediments will become a conduit for water, even when refilled with sediment. This is especially true when pipelines are installed in the excavation. In the recent move of the Southeast Lighthouse, a large tract of land was excavated around the structure. Later the soil was replaced. However, the reorganized glacial sediments no longer retain their water-retarding characteristics. Surface water will now more readily infiltrate the soil. Excess water flowing toward the bluff and into the sediments may accelerate slumping toward the original site of the lighthouse.

RECENT STORM DAMAGE

Slumps and eroded blocks of sediment are highly visible along the Island's coast where bluffs have undergone significant erosion due to storms in recent years. Major storms have increased the rate of mass wasting well above a four feet per year average. In many of the exposed headlands, sand layers have been washed out leaving large cavities around the masses of lower till. Due to the lack of support the more resistant till will slump and the bluff will recede. Overhangs, where the roots hold the soil layer at the surface, fresh slump blocks of till onto the beach, rock falls, deepening gullies, and sediment fans are all visible components of the process of slope readjustment. Since the slope recession is not immediate, we often are not aware of the full extent of storm damage. But the effects, like the loss of land, are nonetheless devastating.

BEACHES

Beach walkers who have observed the Island's shoreline over the years are well aware of the seasonal changes in beach deposits. Those who have gone down to the shore during and after major storms know how the waves vary from day to day. We have witnessed how the beach is eroded and reshaped, and we are increasingly aware of the range of the tides. For example, in recent years more breaking waves riding on high water have plowed into the dunes. In the big storms of the early 1990's, high tides and storm surges cut cliffs on the dunes, excavated bluffs, washed over the causeways at Harbor Pond and Sachem Pond, and undercut roadways on Spring Street and at Settlers Rock.

Generally, the beaches are stripped of sand by early spring. At Mansion and Scotch beaches, where sand covered a wide expanse of beach from the water's edge to the dunes in the previous summer, the sand layer has thinned out by late winter, and the spring beach is all gravel. Close attention to the gravel berm reveals a massive pile of cobbles sorted in size and lined up toward the sea. This gravel terrace has been scalloped by the breaking waves into neat cusps with nearly flat tops and steep ocean-facing slopes. The erosive violence of coastal storms has removed much of the sand layer, exposing the underlying gravels. It has cut a steep beach face, and then mysteriously shaped the gravel bar. The cuspate pattern actually results from the energy generated by the complex geometry of wave direction, spacing and size, as well as the nature of the beach materials and the shape and orientation of sand ridges on the offshore sea bed.

As summer approaches, the sand begins to return. Slowly the gravels disappear beneath the sand sheet; the erratics are gradually submerged, and the beach gets thicker and wider. Winter storm-driven tides that swirled into the dunes are now replaced by a more regular rise and fall of the sea. Only after a seasonable nor'easter can we confirm that a thick sand sheet was again deposited over the gravel bed. Due to the storm, the gravel again pokes out from new gullies cut in the beach face by water running back to the sea, and the waves have carved a terrace into the berm. Where, we might ask, does the sand go in the winter? And where did the gravel come from and where does it go in the summer? Is the sand stored offshore in deep water and then recyled back on the beach by gentle summer seas?

Unfortunately, the answers to these questions are not entirely reassuring. Sand may be stored in offshore beds, but a good portion is lost from the coastal zone because it is carried by bottom currents out to sea, beyond the Island's shallows and into water too deep for it to be reclaimed even by the biggest storm waves. Some fine-grained sand ends up in the harbors and is only retrieved by dredging, while some accretes to the dunes through wind action. Most of the sand for each new season comes from erosion of the bluffs. The greater the erosion, the more the beaches are fed and the healthier they seem to be in mid-summer. Recent coastal storms have generated enough sand to temporarily cover the gravel beaches from Stevens Cove to Dories Cove. But the Island itself is diminished when storms erode the bluffs

and mobilize the sand.   The heavier gravels lag behind
to gradually weather and disintegrate.

Typically, the beach is a complex of landforms and
deposits of sediment of varying sizes, all sorted out by
waves and wind currents from the tidal forebeach to the
back beach dunes (Figure 14). The forebeach extends from
the low tide line landward through the berm, a ridge
above the high tide zone that runs parallel to the
shoreline. Sand accretes to the forebeach and extends
the beach face seaward. At high water, waves wash sand
over the berm. Like the gravels, the sandy berm also
takes on a cuspate form. Offshore, deep waves and
currents reshape the sand sheet of the sea bed into
submarine ridges with intervening swales, an indication
of the wave energy inherent in the water column.
Stronger, taller waves form more impressive breakers to
our eyes, and because of their depth, they have a greater
impact on the sea bed. Magnified by the increase in wave
height during storms, counter currents on the sea floor
carry much of the sand out to sea.

Landward, the back beach consists of a low plain
between the berm and the primary line of sand dunes. A
depression or swale may retain a shallow pond of sea

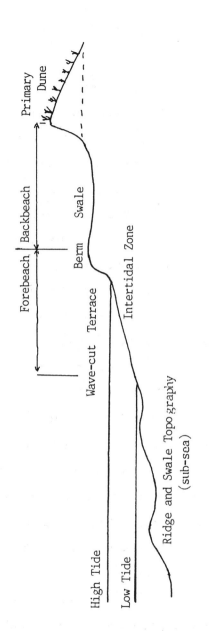

Figure 14. A cross section of a typical beach.

water washed over the berm. As the water level in the pond drops, the surface of the swale may become encrusted with an algal mat growing on the warm, damp sand. Outlets from the ponds are rare, so the water slowly evaporates. With higher sea levels, the back beach is inundated more frequently and high tide washovers flood the dune area.

Along the beach front, the energy of breaking waves creates a zone of coastal erosion and sediment transport parallel to the beach (Figure 15). Because the waves usually reach the beach at an angle, a current is generated that transmits wave energy along the beach. This current, called the longshore current, transports sand in the downstream direction in a process called longshore or littoral drift. Sand from the bluffs near Scotch Beach can reach Mansion Beach on a longshore current from wave sets with a southeast fetch. The current sorts the sand and feeds the beach along the way. Northeast waves carry sand from the northeast bluffs to Crescent Beach. In a similar fashion, sand from the Old Harbor bluffs reaches Ballards Beach, and some of the fine sand winds up at the mouth of the Old Harbor. Tidal action redistributes the sand into the channel, making

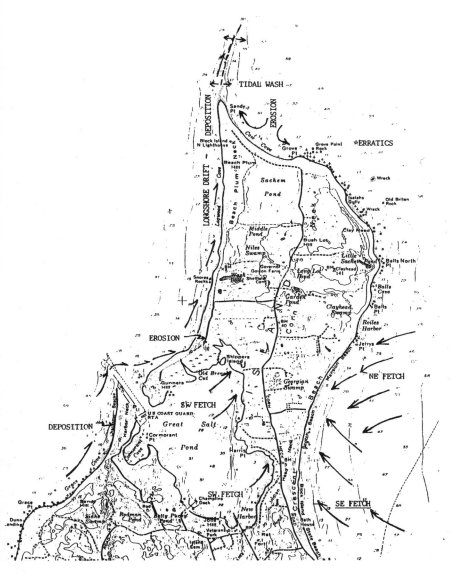

Figure 15. Coastal currents and deposition and erosion areas for northern Block Island.

periodic dredging a necessity. Otherwise, with only small pocket beaches to feed, much of the sediment from the southeast bluffs joins the sands on the continental shelf, representing a direct loss of material from the Island.

On the west side of the Island, the longshore current carries sand eroded from the western bluffs through Sandy Hill northward to Charleston Beach and eventually to Sandy Point. The supply of sand has been great enough that over the thousands of years of erosion of the southerly coast, deposition of sand northward has built up the Island's northwestern beaches and dunes and extended a sand bar from Sandy Point reaching into Block Island Sound. It does not seem likely today that much sand washes to the east side of the Island because the easterly beaches are so rocky. However, in the last century Cow Cove, which was a popular bathing beach on the northeast coast of the Island, may have received some of its sand from the west side. Enough sand could have been carried by the tides across the Sandy Point bar from the west side to nourish this beach. However, much of the sand was removed by storms, including the 1938 hurricane. Now not enough sand is available to nourish this beach, perhaps because Sandy Point has extended farther to the north, and coarse gravel covers the Cow Cove and Grove Point shorelines. This erosion and deposition regime will be reconsidered again when we look at how people have interacted with the development of the coast.

SAND DUNES

   The expanding sand plain of the summer beach promotes another important processes, the accretion of sand dunes. If you have ever tried to sunbathe while a strong wind is blowing you know the sting of moving sand. You might also be aware of how the sand begins to pile up against you. In effect you have become a barrier to the movement of sand, a role more successfully played by inanimate objects. When blowing hard enough, say around one foot per second, wind can move particles ranging from silt to medium-sized sand. Over a year's time, the wind may blow from several directions. However, the net effect of sand movement will be governed by the most consistent winds.

As the sand moves, the grains get blasted by smaller particles and bumped along by larger particles. The sand blasting frosts and rounds the grains, while the varying wind speeds sort the particles by size and weight and moves them downwind. Ultimately, an obstruction like a rock or drift wood forms a barrier, and the sand begins to accumulate. As the deposit grows, it acquires a predictable form; a long, gentle windward slope and a short and steep leeward slope. The sand climbs the gentle slope and collects at the upper edge. When the mass of sand reaches a critical angle, around thirty degrees, it cascades down the short, steep slope. Steady winds and a good supply of sand insure the growth and maintenance of the dunes; excessive winds and a short supply of sand cause erosion; a balance of wind and sand will stabilize the dunes and allow vegetation to grow on the gentle windward slope. Close inspection of the dune shows that wind ripples on the gentle windward surface are dune forms in miniature, all lined up in parallel rows by the prevailing wind. As the wind blows, the sand grains migrate downwind from ripple to ripple.

Layer upon layer of sand accumulates in this way, eventually building dunes that gain heights of tens of feet. At Scotch and Town beaches the dunes rise to about thirty feet above sea level; Beach Plum Hill near the North Light is nearly fifty feet high. When dunes erode, the lighter mineral fraction, mostly quartz sand, is removed, and a lag deposit of heavy mineral sand including magnetite, garnet and other minerals heavier than quartz, forms a reddish-black layer. Like the quartz sands, the heavy minerals were once part of the crystalline rock fragments brought to the Island by the glaciers. Even these tiny particles can be specific to one source area and an asset in studies of provenance.

We have to remember dune sand is finer grained than beach sand, and ocean waves are more powerful than the wind. When the sea's energy is expended against the dunes, they virtually melt away, reminding us how fragile and temporary they are.

SEA LEVEL RISE

Left to its own devices, the Island would seem to be eroding on the east, south and southwest sides, because of the direction of energy from the ocean currents, and growing along the northwest coast. But now, as a spectre of things to come, the net loss of land has become more of a reality. We are increasingly aware of the winter losses along the coast, as the bluffs recede toward cliffside houses, and winter beach erosion exceeds summer resupply of sand. Has some new factor tipped the seemingly predictable balance of beach processes? The answer is a firm, yes. In fact, a couple of powerful influences have now asserted control over the destiny of the coastline.

On the one hand, people have made a major impact on the coast, building in sensitive areas and dredging and rearranging the face of the land with little awareness of geological processes or environmental consequences. On the other, the world-wide effects of changing climate, also a consequence of destructive environmental practices, have had a pronounced impact on sea level. There is considerable scientific evidence to show that global warming, underway since the end of the "Little Ice Age", a natural cold climate interval that lasted from the fifteenth to the nineteenth centuries, has been accelerated by an increase of carbon dioxide in the atmosphere. This increase is a side effect of the extravagant use of fossil fuels since the industrial revolution. Higher levels of gases and particulate matter in the atmosphere cause the "greenhouse effect," the mechanism in which the earth's heat is trapped by the atmosphere. As a consequence, warmer climate has caused glaciers to melt and the level of the sea to rise on a global scale.

One prominent theory of the cause of ice ages and warm intervals deals with cyclic and differential heating and cooling of the earth due to change in the tilt of the earth's axis, the shape of the earth's orbit around the sun, and the distance of the earth from the sun. While the orbit varies from nearly circular to an elongate ellipse, the optimum-for warmth position has the earth's axis vertical and the earth closest to the sun. It takes about ninety-six thousand years for the earth's orbit to change from elliptical to circular and back, about the same duration as a major glacial and interglacial cycle. The axial tilt cycle takes about forty-one thousand years, about the same as a glacial subcycle, with half that time, twenty thousand years for the interval from the last glacial to the present warm episode.

Along with these comparable astronomical events and

terrestrial climates, short-term, cold-warm cycles are attributed to the exchange of oceanic heat from the southern to the northern oceans via deep-water ocean circulation. In addition, the onset of Pleistocene glacial cycles overall is thought to be related to the uplift of the western North American plateaus during the Tertiary Period which altered global atmospheric circulation. To all of these interacting agencies we can add atmospheric pollution aggrevated by increasing carbon dioxide, other gases and volcanic eruptions. The result is a heightened greenhouse effect that increasingly warms the atmosphere and prolongs and intensifies the interstadial climate. Researchers have already noted increases in the global heat budget, changes in plant and animal distributions, particularly in the life of the southern ocean, and most importantly the increased melting of glacial ice that has resulted in the rise of the sea.

The major effect of higher sea level- a worldwide phenomenon- will be to inundate the present coastline. Coastal cities will be flooded, beaches and dunes will disappear along with some islands, and more rivers will be drowned. Some tide gauges show mean sea level rising about one eighth of an inch per year, or about one foot every one hundred years, a rate that matches the measured rate of salt marsh growth in this region. In three hundred years sea level may have risen as much as three feet.

What does this much sea level rise look like to us? Try a simple test at the beach when the tide is high: imagine a water level three feet higher; then project that level to the dunes, bluffs, and seaside buildings. It is not hard to see how much of the shoreline would be covered with water. On the topographic map, the new shoreline can be approximated by a line drawn between the water and the first contour line at ten feet above mean sea level (Figure 16). The new shoreline would bisect Block Island: beaches would be submerged, dunes eroded, waves would be pounding against the bluffs, and the jetties that protect the harbors would be almost awash. Of course, this process is slow going like all geological processes. We do not notice the change until its effects are critical. Over time, the slow rise of the sea will cause coastal erosion farther inland. The model assumes that the fragile dunes will essentially melt away, and in time somebody else will have waterfront property.

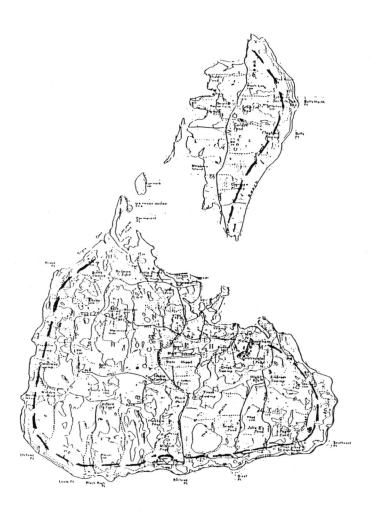

Figure 16. The projected perimeter of Block Island in 2300 AD based on sea level rise to the five foot level; dashed lines represent potential additional bluff erosion by 2300 AD.

One of the best examples of our involvement with the present coastline is in maintaining the harbors. The jetty that has protected the opening into Great Salt Pond for much of this century has also changed the western shore. It has trapped or delayed the northward movement of sand from the southwest bluffs. As a consequence, Harbor Neck has been widened to form Charleston Beach, a sand spit nearly one third of a mile wide with ten foot-high sand dunes and a shoreline close to the seaward end of the jetty.

On the north side of the inlet, Gunners Hill and the low bluffs to the north are eroding, and the beach is being cut eastward into a deep crescentic salient. This is because the jetty deflects the longshore current into this part of the coast. Offshore, former marshland is submerged below the transgressing sea. We can appreciate how the current by-passes the jetty and erodes the beach and bluffs. It leaves some sand in the channel, but it erodes sand from the beach north of the jetty. This sand moves northward toward Logwood Cove where it nourishes the beach and supplies the dunes of Beach Plum Neck and Sandy Point. Subsea data show the extension of Sands Point to the north, and from the topographic map we can see that Sachem Pond and Middle Pond owe their existence to the build up of Beach Plum Neck, a barrier beach that has cut these ponds off from Block Island Sound.

Rising sea level will increase the amount of sand in this procession by increasing the erosion of the bluffs. For a time Beach Plum Neck and Sandy Point will continue to grow, at least until the sea drowns the beach and floods inland (remember the three foot level) to cut new bluffs against the Corn Neck hillside. At this time, the ponds - Sachem, Middle and Great Salt ponds, will join the Sound. Harbor Neck and Gunners Hill will be small islands, and Corn Neck will be separated from the south of the Island.

HYDROGEOLOGY AND WATER RESOURCES

A number of years ago at a meeting of concerned Block Island citizens, a visiting geologist was trying to caution residents against overdevelopment, citing a limited drinking-water supply as an important restricting factor. The geologist reviewed the hydrogeology of the Island and the nature of the subsurface water resource, emphasizing the fact that the only source of water supply was rainfall and concluding with a discussion of the relationship between water supply and population.

After a respectful time, one of the more influential of the citizens countered the scientific evidence with what was believed to be the gospel of Island water supply, namely that the source was an underground river that originated in northern New England as pure mountain spring water. This river flowed deep beneath the Island providing an unlimited supply of fresh, well-filtered drinking water to its residents.

Unfortunately, this bountiful resource does not exist. All of the fresh water of the Island comes from rainfall, and it is precariously stored at the surface in ponds and below ground in the sediments that form natural reservoirs called aquifers. Furthermore, the aquifers are not that conveniently tapped and are not adequately monitored. In fact the aquifers are subject to a great variety of abuses by "out-of-sight, out-of-mind" waste-disposal practices that pre-empt a zero-pollution agenda.

The public water supply is derived from Sands Pond and from deep wells that penetrate iron-oxide and clay-rich Cretaceous sediments over two hundred feet below the surface. This water requires special chemical treatment to achieve drinking water status. Prior to the upgrading of the water system, the product in the pipeline was close to unusable. It was badly in need of purification, a new water storage tank and regular testing. Only a complex water treatment schedule and better storage and transmission facilities have been able to improve the quality of Town water. However, the improvements can not increase rainfall, the sole source of fresh water, and in drought years the public water supply is seriously inadequate.

The rest of the Island's population is served by ponds and private wells dependent on the hydrologic characteristics of the Island's geologic formations. The hydrogeology of the Island is determined by glacial and preglacial strata that consist mainly of unconsolidated sediments of varying grain size, sorting, compaction and chemical properties. As explained earlier, the glacial deposits are the result of two separate glaciations. They range from glacial till to outwash and include structural distortions due to ice-contact deformation.

In general, the superimposed glacial drifts are comprised of tills separated by outwash, all with different water transmitting characteristics. The older, lower till is clayey, compact and less able to transmit water or permit water infiltration. It supports surface water in ponds and marshes, and below the surface, it acts as a confining layer for groundwater that accumulates in the overlying sediments. The younger, upper drift, which forms the morainal topography of the Island, is sandy and less compact. It more readily allows the passage of water, and it provides a source of near-surface water. The glacial deposits are underlain by layers of Cretaceous sediments of both marine and coastal plain origin that may or may not contain potable water.

The fresh water contained in the sedimentary aquifers is derived from rainfall, but near the coast salt water

97

has infiltrated the sediments. Rainfall has averaged forty five inches per year over the long term, but it can drop to thirty inches per year during dry years. On a monthly basis, average long-term rainfall ranges from a low of about two and one half inches to a high of four inches. The low, or water-deficient months, are from June to September, which coincide with the Island's seasonal high population and high water use.

Rain falling on the earth's surface tends to seek lower elevations. Initially running overland as a thin sheet, water begins to cut into the soil to form gullies; gullies merge into stream channels of increasing depth and width before reaching a pond, a bluff or the sea. Erosion becomes evident after a rain because sand flows out of driveways onto paved roads and plumes of muddy water cloud the ponds. Much of the surface water seeps into the porous ground, the rest is taken up by plants or it evaporates.

Water that infiltrates the soil eventually finds the open spaces between the sediment grains in the glacial deposits. These deposits vary in their ability to hold or to transmit water. Most of the layers are porous to some degree, that is, there are open spaces between the grains; they are also more or less permeable in that they allow water to flow from pore space to pore space. Those layers that are relatively impermeable, or of low permeability, impede the flow of water. Aquifers are layers that are porous, relatively permeable, and have attained a significant build up or saturation of water. They are bounded above and below by confining layers, generally consisting of relatively impermeable strata (Figure 17).

The three-part nature of this geological sandwich enables us to produce the water by drilling into the porous and permeable aquifer, sealing the well above and below it, and pumping out the fresh water. The main aquifer for the Island is a hydrologically continuous, general zone of saturation located in the vicinity of sea level. Groundwater is also stored in perched water tables at higher elevations, and these may be unconfined aquifers.

Water is transmitted through the aquifers, depending on the nature of the materials and the slope of the layers, at a rate of flow around two hundred to three hundred feet per day. This means that not all of the rainwater that falls on the Island takes up permanent

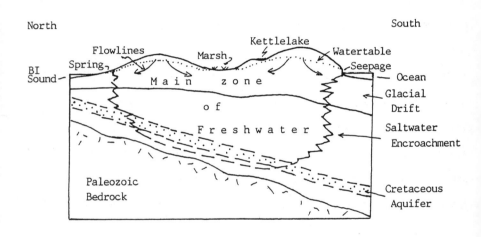

Figure 17.   A generalized cross section of Block Island aquifers.

residence in the subsurface geology. The Island's strata slowly leak water from the bluffs, from surface seeps and springs into ponds and marshes, and from below sea level into the sea. Seeps provide sustenance for aquatic life, and springs with their mystical healing properties have been a popular source of drinking water. The relatively impermeable lower till acts as a confining layer for some perched water and may support ponds, which are important reservoirs of fresh water. Fresh Pond, which has been suggested as a back-up water supply for the Town, has a drainage area of around two hundred acres, and one foot of pond water represents about one million gallons of stored water. This is obviously a resource that should be protected. Small ponds are known to dry up by August, while the shores of larger ponds widen to expose iron-stained boulders.

Island wide, water recharge from a good rain can add hundreds of thousands of gallons of water to the aquifers. A map of the water table shows that the main zone of saturation includes a layer of sediment that varies between thirty feet above sea level and fifteen feet below. South of Great Salt Pond, groundwater flow follows the configuration of the topographic highs and lows, so that recharge of the aquifers begins near highs, flows away from topographic or groundwater divides and into the aquifers. However, the direction of groundwater flow north of Great Salt Pond is generally toward the axis of Corn Neck in a north-northeasterly direction due to the slope of the lower drift. The general flow is complicated by the shape of the lower till surface, and by the chaotic arrangement of irregular blocks of lower till, Cretaceous sediments, and structural features like slump blocks and fault lines. The thrusted Cretaceous and lower till blocks have low water-bearing properties and can result in dry wells when the blocks are stacked above each other.

The Cretaceous sediments are rich in iron oxide that can leach into the groundwater. Water flow around the layers of low permeability may be channeled into pipe-like configurations in permeable sediments where iron oxide may be precipitated as a thick crust. Around gravel it can form a solid conglomerate of rock debris cemented with an iron oxide crust. At Pots and Kettles near Clay Head, several red conglomerate piping structures protrude from the outwash in the bluff onto the beach; the cemented gravel is more resistant to wave

erosion than the surrounding sediment.   Even through
recent pounding by storm-driven waves, the groundwater
pipes at Pots and Kettles can still be seen on the beach
below the bluffs.

GROUNDWATER QUALITY

The groundwater of Block Island can be somewhat acid and corrosive. Analyses of water samples from around the Island have shown distinct trends in acidity, chloride, and salt content due to salt water encroachment, as well as iron, sulfate and several other compounds. Acidity and high chloride may be related in some areas. When demand for fresh water increases, high pumping rates tend to draw the fresh water level down, reversing groundwater flow and pulling salt water inland across the zone of mixing, or diffusion. Wells closest to the coast will produce water with high chloride, or salt, content; the chloride level in sea water ranges between 1,000 and 10,000 milligrams per liter (mg/l).

Low chloride levels around 30 mg/l are considered normal, and are found in the interior in areas around Beacon Hill and Old Town, for example. Chlorides are higher in the commercial district around Old Harbor, New Harbor, and in residential areas around Great Salt Pond and along the coastlines where readings above 100 mg/l are recorded. Wash Pond adjacent to the Transfer Station tested at nearly 200 mg/l of chloride in the old landfill days, while Sachem Pond was around 40 mg/l.

High levels of iron- well over 3.8 mg/l- may be associated with a water source in Cretaceous sediments, either in the deep Cretaceous aquifer or in water perched on masses of Cretaceous sediments. Iron in these layers is leached out by groundwater flow. High iron and sulfate are also found in some ponds where biological activity causes low oxygen levels, reducing conditions and precipitation of iron compounds. In this setting, bacteria fix iron and sulfur to clay and other compounds to produce the precipitates.

Sources of groundwater pollution are tied to discharge of residential and commercial waste water, and are often the result of defective septic systems. Illegal dumping of waste water, household and industrial chemicals, fuels, oil, detergents, and garbage into septic systems, or behind the barn, or in a pond is a leading source of groundwater contamination. Leaching of such contaminants into the Island's limited water supply can be a long-lasting process and have serious impact on water quality. Many of the compounds are not biodegradable and are not filtered out in transit through the sediments. Thus, the water may remain toxic indefinitely.

In a sole source aquifer, slow groundwater recharge and a very limited flow-through water mechanism means that toxic chemicals are not flushed out of the system. They stay in the aquifer and are concentrated over time. In other words, they do not go away. For example, the Island's former landfill and sludge dump have generated a north-flowing, toxic groundwater plume that will probably continue to affect aquifer water quality for years. Higher than normal amounts of colliform bacteria, iron, nitrate, sodium, sulfate, lead, zinc, manganese, and chromium, as well as high acidity, and very high electrical conductivity- as much as thirty times normal- have all been associated with groundwater and pond water near the landfill.

Due to geologic constraints, the plume is moving slowly northward, rather than westward into Block Island Sound or downward into the mysterious depths. Flow is more horizontal, following the surface of the relatively impermeable lower drift, and finding its way through lenses of outwash sands into the ponds and groundwater to the north. At the height of open pit dumping in the 1980's, leachate negatively impacted groundwater as far north as Sachem Pond, where the water was quite acid-

recording a pH of 3.8, where a pH of 7.0 is neutral. By comparison, the pH of Great Salt Pond is around 6.0. Since the termination of open pit dumping around 1987, tests have not been regularly conducted and the post-dumping history of the plume is not known.

In view of the pollution potential, the Island's fresh water supply, although proclaimed sufficient in a recent United States Geological Survey study, should be closely monitored- an occasional water study can not follow possible trends of contamination or locate point sources of pollution. Such sources, like defective septic systems, contaminated water wells, leaking storage tanks, and open dumping and storage of toxic substances should be identified and corrected. We all need to improve on our own practices, increase our conservation methods, and aim for a zero-based pollution goal for Block Island's water supply.

FIELD TRIPS

In the context of geologic time, which covers over four and one half billion years, the formation of Block Island is like the blink of an eye. It took only about two thousand years between twenty-two thousand and twenty thousand ago for glacial advance and deposition of the terminal and recessional moraines that make up Block Island. Then, between twelve thousand years ago and the present, sea level rise and coastal erosion shaped the moraine and created the Island. Consequently, the variety and form of glacial and postglacial features, readily available for study, is excellent. These features range from deposits and landforms to contorted strata. They are very well represented and nowhere as well exposed as in the bluffs of Block Island or on the Island's surface. These features are accessible by car and bicycle along the roadways and on hikes along the beaches and trails.

Field trips to various parts of the Island are described in this section. Each trip has scenic views and opportunities for taking pictures. The descriptions include maps, explanations and sketches of geologic features (Figure 18). Distances along the routes are approximated in tenths of miles and geologic sites are keyed to the place names referenced on the United States Geological Survey, Block Island, R. I., 7.5' Topographic Quadrangle. Segments of this map are reproduced here for each of the excursions. The map is available from the United States Geological Survey, Reston, Va. 22092.

Because the Island is already greatly diminished by the unrelenting forces of natural erosion, we ask that you do not collect samples of rocks, plants or endangered insect species, or disturb nesting birds.

EXCURSION GEOLOGY

The geology of the Island, as viewed in its many bluffs, is characterized by intense glacial deformation. The exposures in the bluffs allow us to examine the results of deformation in wide-open cross sections along the direction of ice movement, roughly north to south, simply by walking along the north-south beaches. Or we can see the effects of deformation perpendicular to the direction of movement by viewing the east-west cuts in

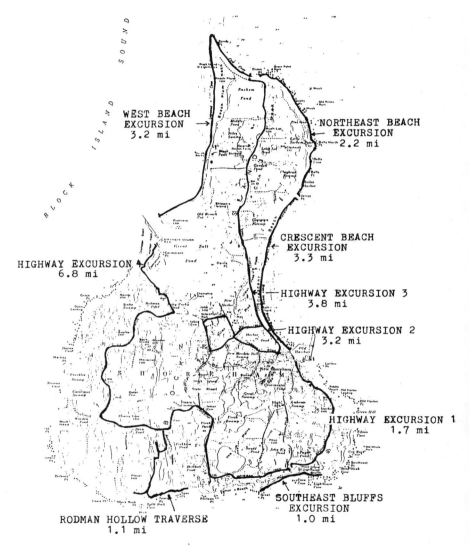

WEST BEACH
EXCURSION
3.2 mi

NORTHEAST BEACH
EXCURSION
2.2 mi

CRESCENT BEACH
EXCURSION
3.3 mi

HIGHWAY EXCURSION 4
6.8 mi

HIGHWAY EXCURSION 3
3.8 mi

HIGHWAY EXCURSION 2
3.2 mi

HIGHWAY EXCURSION 1
1.7 mi

RODMAN HOLLOW TRAVERSE
1.1 mi

SOUTHEAST BLUFFS
EXCURSION
1.0 mi

Figure 18. The location of field excursions described in
the text.

the southern bluffs.

The major stratigraphic units in the bluffs are the upper and lower glacial drifts, both of which contain tills, outwash and lake beds. They are distinguished first by their relative position, normally the older, lower drift below, and the younger, upper drift above. Next, color is a basic characteristic: the older drift is in shades of gray, the younger in yellow-browns, both depending on mineral content and provenance. The upper drift is rich in granitic rock debris owing to its northwesterly source area in granitic terrain. The till stones and erratics are lumped together here as "granitic" in composition. This is a category of convenience that can include granite, granite gneiss, pegmatite and quartzite, rock types with similar color and mineral content. The lower drift has more of the dark-colored rocks from the mainland to the northeast, including darker-colored gneisses, amphibolite schists, phyllites, metaconglomerates and coal. In this section, the geologic descriptions may cite "granitic gravel" or "dark-colored till stones" as indications of the presence of the upper or lower drifts.

The oldest sedimentary deposits seen in the

excursions are sands, clays, and gravels of Cretaceous age which appear as masses of sediment thrusted into the moraines by the last glacier. The lower drift unit may consist of glacial till, often a variety known as lodgement or basal till deposited and compressed beneath the glacier. It may either be in place or deformed and ice shoved, or as ripped-up blocks detached from the main body of drift and thrusted into and engulfed by the outwash of the younger drift. Lake sediments in the lower drift include banded clays that appear in the exposures as tightly-folded, thin-bedded layers.

In the upper drift, the outwash may be gently sloping or deformed and steeply inclined with thrusted blocks of Cretaceous and lower drift. The most common upper drift till is meltout till, which as the name implies is partly washed by meltwater. Meltout till generally overlies the outwash and varies in thickness from beds to thin boulder-rich layers. Tills interbedded with the outwash are flow tills, a variety that flowed as a layer from the ice along with the sand and gravel. An impressive sequence of sand and clay layers may be part of a delta that formed in a proglacial lake during glacial recession. Postglacial wind-blown silts, called loess, often form a layer capping the glacial sequences. The loess may have old soil profiles, paleosols, buried under more recent sand dunes at the top of most bluffs. Due to glacial deformation, the bluff geology can be difficult to decipher. At every point and cove the deposits exhibit differing thicknesses and variations in structural complication, and these can change as coastal erosion and slumping remove sediment and reveal new interdrift relationships.

The beach deposits, excluding the flotsam, are the result of the interaction of coastal processes and the erosion of the bluffs. On the beach below the bluffs, we can see berms of coarse gravel, slump blocks with masses of sediment and vegetation, and slides of sediment from high up the cliffs, including sand washed down the gullies by rain.

Overland excursions reveal the topography of glacial deposition and recession. The surface sediments are more apt to reflect the granitic character of the upper drift. However, the terrain of glacial recession with its meltwater channels, proglacial lakes and ice-contact deposits is as distinctive as the kame and kettle or hummocky topography of the end moraines. The moraines have crests or ridge lines and slopes, the proximal slope facing the glacier and the distal slope facing away. In addition to these glacial features, landforms created by a readvance of the last glacier, the recent effects of erosion and submergence of the coastline, the accretion of some beaches, and the deposition of recent sand dunes all combine to make the overland geology as fascinating as that of the bluffs.

Highway Excursion 1. Mohegan Bluffs to Water Street, Old Harbor, via Southeast Road and Spring Street, 1.7 miles (Figure 19). This trip provides a good introduction to the landscape of an end moraine impacted by a large block of Cretaceous sediments thrusted southward along the Island's southeastern shore.

0.0 miles. Mohegan Bluffs (see Southeast Bluffs Excursion for the geology of the bluffs). Proceed eastward and then northward, over morainal topography. There are several kettles on the distal (south) slope of the Beacon Hill Moraine, a recessional moraine of the last glaciation. The terminal moraine was deposited well south of Block Island and the Southeast Bluffs and has

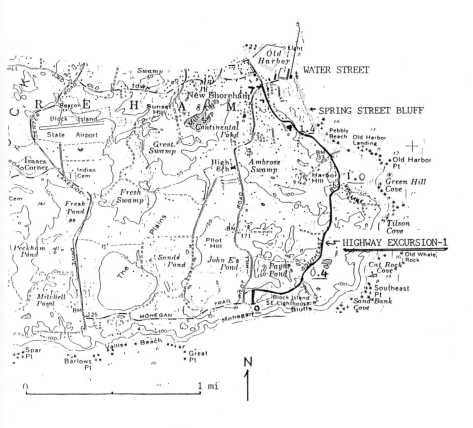

WATER STREET

← SPRING STREET BLUFF

← HIGHWAY EXCURSION-1

N

1 mi

Figure 19.   Highway Excursion 1. Mohegan Bluffs to Water
             Street.

been substantially eroded by the rising sea. Its remnants, mostly erratics, now lie below sea level well off the south coast of the Island and have been encountered by fishermen and scuba divers.

0.4 miles. At the crest of Southeast Road on the left side, the west shoulder of the road is cut into a hill (probably a kame) exposing granitic gravel of the younger drift.

0.4 to 1.0 miles. The road descends over morainal topography in a northerly direction along the proximal slope (north) of the Beacon Hill Moraine to Hull Lane. Looking north from Hull Lane, a flat topographic terrace extends north-south between the road and the coast and Old Harbor. The road traverses the upper surface of the terrace adjacent to the hillslope on the west. The terrace is mainly underlain by a tabular block of Cretaceous strata that was thrust southward by the ice, parallel to the upland and into the moraine. A postglacial wetland overlies the Cretaceous beds.

1.4 miles. East of the Spring House Hotel, water from a spring has cut a small channel eastward across the terrace, which also supports a pond (on the right hand side of the road) filled with aquatic vegetation. This pond and the water table are perched on impermeable lake clays that, in turn, are underlain by Cretaceous clay.

At this point walk down to the beach level to see the stratigraphy of this Spring Street bluff (Figure 20). It consists of several feet of Cretaceous sediments, including light gray clay overlain by dark gray clay with lenses of coal-like lignite and separate masses of white clayey sand and gravel. The presence of coal as a potential fuel was intriguing enough to early settlers that attempts were made to exploit the deposit, but with little success. Glacial outwash and meltout till and a layer of postglacial loess cover the Cretaceous beds. There are also the remaining beds of a postglacial pond and peat bog above the glacial deposits. These include lake clays and a thick layer of brown peat that are the postglacial ancestors of the present pond. Occasionally slumps of peat and outwash partly obscure the bluff geology, including the Cretaceous beds. Based on pollen analysis, the Cretaceous lignite is equivalent to the Raritan Formation of Upper Cretaceous age in New Jersey and Long Island. The pollen in the postglacial peat date this layer to the time before twelve thousand years ago when spruce forests covered the Island following the

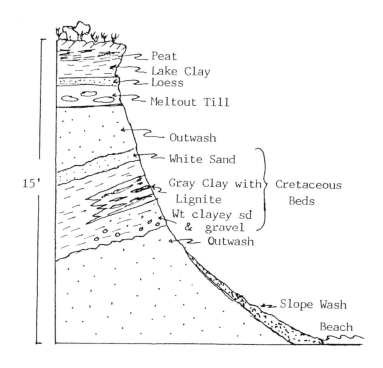

Figure 20a. Geology of the Spring Street bluff.

Figure 20b. Outwash above Cretaceous lignite and clay in the Spring Street bluff section.

retreat of the ice.

1.4 to 1.7 miles. Proceed northward along Spring Street, cutting across the moraine and then descending into Water Street at the statue of Rebeccah. Small hills to the south and west of the statue around the Water Street area are drumlin-shaped and were sculptured by a readvance of the ice during the recession of the last glacier. Before land filling, marshes formed in the low areas between the hills.

Highway Excursion 2. The Drumlin Field of Harbor Pond (Figure 21). Block Island Post Office and return, 3.2 miles. This excursion takes you through a scenic panorama of elliptical hills surrounded by salt pond and marshes. The hills are drumlins that were sculptured by readvancing ice that overrode existing late Wisconsinan glacial deposits.

0.0 miles. The route of this excursion makes a loop or figure eight, starting at the Ocean Avenue (Harbor Road on the topographic map)- Corn Neck Road intersection and proceeding westward. As you cross the flat area beyond the Post Office, note the small drumlins forming the local landscape, for example, the hill to the south (on

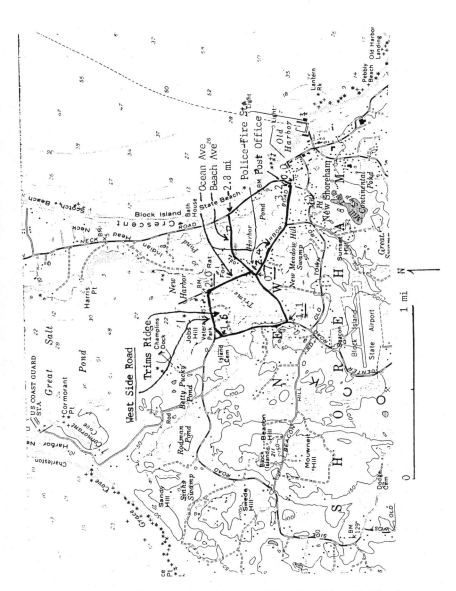

Figure 21a. Highway Excursion 2. The drumlin field of Harbor Pond

121

Figure 21b. Indian Head Neck: a north (on right) to
south profile of a drumlin.

the left) at Mill Pond, the hill to the north with a cluster of red roofed buildings, the hill at the Block Island Power Company, and the hills around the intersection of Ocean Avenue and Beach Avenue at the Police Station-Fire House. To the north of the road on the right, Harbor Pond has filled in and around the small hills. The red-roofed drumlin has a classical shape: steep to the north, the direction from which the ice advanced, and tailing off southward in a gentle, fluted slope. As a botanical aside, the park on the north side of Ocean Avenue opposite the Power Company is bordered along the road by several Osage Orange trees, an exotic planting for a New England island. This tree species, which is resistant to disease, insects and drought, produces very tough wood and was originally used by the Osage people of Oklahoma as a living stockade for their livestock.

0.7 miles. Turn left (southwest) at the next intersection and follow Beach Avenue to Center Road. New Meadow Hill Swamp on your left was also once part of Harbor Pond and a link with Trims Pond but was cut off by both Ocean Avenue and Beach Avenue. Drumlins form the upland adjacent to the road.

1.1 miles. Turn right (north) on to Center Road and proceed toward West Side Road. The road crosses the slope of the moraine which has been sculpted into drumlins, including the Island Cemetery on the left.

1.6 miles. Turn right (east) on to West Side Road at Veterans Park. Trims Ridge on the right and Jobs Hill, site of The Oar Restaurant, are drumlins. Jobs Hill was cut by storm erosion and a view from the beach reveals stratified sediments and meltout till.

2.0 miles. Right (south) on Ocean Avenue. Cross the small drumlin at Fort Island and Trims Pond bridge and proceed to the top of the hill (another drumlin) at the Police Station-Fire House.

2.4 miles. Go left (northeast) on Beach Avenue. Cross an elongate drumlin and the Harbor Pond Bridge on the way to Corn Neck Road. From the bridge note on the right the picturesque views of Harbor Pond to the southwest bordered by the Ocean Avenue drumlins. From the other side of the bridge is a view to the north of Indian Head Neck with its Victorian-style cottages (see Highway Excursion 3 along Corn Neck Road).

2.9 miles. Turn right (south) on Corn Neck Road, onto a causeway built on fill over the sand bar, geologically a tombolo, which connects the north and south land masses of Block Island. Recent dunes are on the left (east) as is a drumlin with commercial buildings just before the intersection with Ocean Avenue at the Post Office. **3.2 miles.** Intersection with Ocean Avenue.

Highway Excursion 3. Corn Neck Road to Cow Cove, 3.8 miles (Figure 22). Glacial recession and the Corn Neck Moraine. The last glacier retreated northward from the Beacon Hill Moraine, opening a proglacial lake in its wake. Outwash and meltout till covered the deglaciated surface, and lake-bottom varves accumulated for about one hundred years. Subsequently, a brief cooling trend caused the ice to reverse its movement. The glacier readvanced over the terrain, deforming the lake sediments and sculpturing drumlins in the morainal surface. Corn Neck Road provides a view of the landforms of glacial readvance and recession, while the adjoining beach walks (Northeast Beach Excursion and Crescent Beach Excursion) reveal the underlying geology related to these events. **0.0 miles.** Start at the corner of Dodge Street and Corn Neck Road; proceed north on Corn Neck Road. A drumlin on the east (right) side of road gives way to low dunes. The

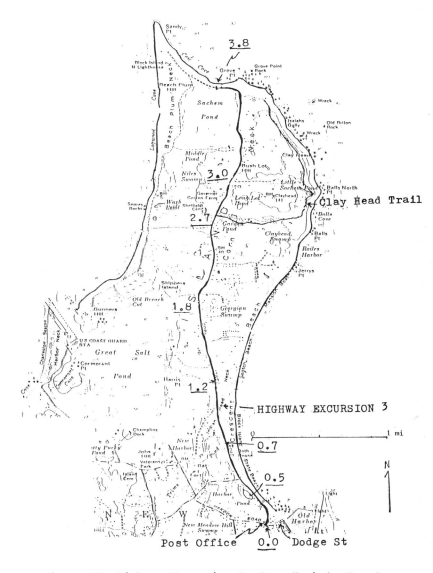

Figure 22. Highway Excursion 3. Corn Neck to Cow Cove.

road is on a causeway constructed over a tombolo connecting north and south Block Island. Storms frequently cut into the underpinnings of the road, exposing bouldery fill and barrels filled with rock.

0.3 miles. The view to west (left) is of drumlins formed during glacial readvance. To the east are dunes over the fill.

0.5 miles. The pond on the left, south of the Boat Works (which is also on a small drumlin) was once an arm of Harbor Pond prior to infilling. At one time it was used as a dump. Recently, the site was restored to that of a landscaped wetland.

0.6 miles. High, shrub-covered dunes border the east side of road.

0.7 miles. To the west (left) stands Indian Head Neck, decorated with green and white Victorian-style cottages. The hill is an elongate ridge with the profile of a drumlin. It was cut into glacial lake sediments comprised of rhythmically-banded fine sands, silts and clays (also called glacial varves). To the east (right) near Town Beach, the dunes rise ten to twenty feet above sea level. In addition to the removal of dunes for construction of the pavilion, the remaining dunes are scarred by foot paths that have been widened by wind erosion. Blowouts (wind excavations) in these erosion scars have decimated the dunes.

1.2 miles. Scotch Beach. A view of Great Salt Pond to west (left). The road begins to rise on the morainal topography of the distal slope of the Corn Neck Moraine. The stone walls that line the roadway and outline adjacent fields were built during colonial land clearing. The walls are mostly of granite and granite gneiss boulders, the surface deposits of the last glaciation. Hummocky topography dominates the landscape of the moraine from here to Sachem Pond with numerous kettles, ponds and swamps in areas of poor drainage.

1.8 miles. Mitchell Farm. A photo-opportunity: a landscape with gambrel barn and cows.

2.6 miles. West Beach Road, the road to the transfer station, is on the left; at its west end it connects with the West Beach Excursion. Note the three foot bank of loess at the entrance.

2.7 miles. Clay Head Trail connector on right. This trail connects with the Northeast Beach Excursion at Roiles Harbor. Along the distal slope, Corn Neck Road blocks the drainage of several small streams forming wetlands.

2.9 miles. A deep erosion gully here is a former east to west stream channel.

3.0 miles. The crest of Corn Neck Moraine atop Bush Lot Hill provides excellent westerly views (to the left) of Beach Plum Neck and Block Island Sound. Descend northward along the proximal slope of the moraine. Views to the north are of Sachem Pond, the North Light, the Cow Cove barrier beach and Block Island Sound.

3.4 miles. The road turns west on the north side of Sachem Pond and continues to Settlers Rock parking lot; the road is on a causeway built on the barrier beach.

3.8 miles. Cow Cove on the north side of the road was once a sandy bathing beach. Coastal storms early in the twentieth century stripped away the sand, leaving the remnant glacial gravels. The Northeast Beach Excursion begins here.

Highway Excursion 4. Mohegan Bluffs to Harbor Neck, site of the Coast Guard Station and Charleston Beach, 6.8 miles, via Mohegan Trail, Rodman Hollow, Cooneymus Road, West Side Road and Champlins Road (formerly Coast Guard Road) (Figure 23). This trip provides a long traverse

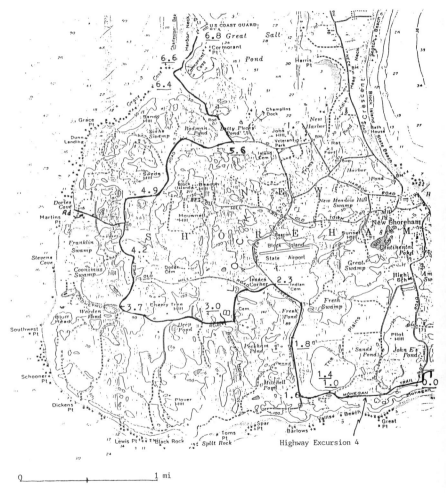

Figure 23a. Highway Excursion 4. Mohegan Bluffs to Harbor
Neck.

130

Figure 23b. A kettle lake and bog on West Side Road.

across the Island from east to west, and then south to north, revealing morainal topography and wetlands, along with features of glacial deposition, retreat and readvance, and beach processes along Harbor Neck.

0.0 miles. Proceed westward on Mohegan Trail from Mohegan Bluffs parking lot, crossing morainal topography and several kettle ponds. Small wetlands on the left near the bluffs may be sag ponds on the back slopes of slump blocks.

0.7 miles. The road cuts across a small kettle with abundant aquatic vegetation.

1.0 miles. A kettle pond on south (left) side of road. The flat plain to north on the right (The Plains) is a former glacial lake bed filled with fine-grained lake sediment.

1.4 miles. The bluffs south of the intersection with Lakeside Drive are slump blocks, some with wetlands in sags (sag ponds).

1.6 miles. Turn right (north) on Lakeside Drive. The view to the west (left) includes Peckham Pond, a kettle pond slowly filling with vegetation.

1.8 miles. On tne left is the south end of Fresh Pond, a large pond in a glacial meltwater channel. A ridge of moraine borders the pond on the west and north. Surface deposits consist of bouldery meltout till of the late Wisconsinan glaciation. Large erratics are embedded in the hillside.

2.3 miles. Turn left on to Cooneymus Road at Isaacs Corner. The road curves around a small hill- probably a kame- and then turns southwest near the intersection with Old Mill Road.

2.8 miles. Sharp right turn.

3.0 miles. Rodman Hollow Overlook (see the Rodman Hollow Traverse). Cooneymus Road cuts across the Rodman Hollow channel. North of the road on the right is a flat glacial lake plain underlain by fine-grained lake sediments. The valley of the meltwater channel to the north heads in the distal slope of the Beacon Hill Moraine. Rodman Hollow to the south (left) of the road occupies a meltwater channel overdeepened in three areas by large ice blocks. These depressions, or kettles, formed when the ice melted. The curve of the channel shows where meltwater flowed over and around the ice blocks and against the glacial drift of the channel walls. Kames border the roadway. Continue westward on Cooneymus Road through morainal topography with occasional kettle ponds.

3.7 miles. Turn right at the intersection with West Side
Road. A deep kettle can be seen to southwest (left), and
hummocky topography of Cherry Tree Hill rises to the
northeast on the right. The kettle is fed, in part, by
a perched-water spring. Ascend the distal slope of the
Beacon Hill Moraine through the granitic surficial
deposits of the last glaciation.

4.2 miles. Excellent views of Block Island Sound to the
west at the intersection Old Mill Road and at the sharp
left turn near the church, and of the coastal wetlands,
Coonimus and Franklin swamps. On a clear day, you can
see Montauk Point which has bluffs very similar to Block
Island's Mohegan Bluffs.

4.5 miles. Dories Cove Road. The crest of the Beacon
Hill Moraine can be seen to the northeast.

4.8 miles. A borrow pit on the right side of road, south
of the Beacon Hill Road intersection, reveals the
stratigraphy of the moraine. The excavation exposes
fine-grained glacial lake beds and flow till at the base.
These lake beds may have originated as a kame delta in
contact with the glacier. These beds are topped by about
forty feet of outwash with meltout till at the top. High

134

angle faults in these sediments indicate slumping and collapse after the melting of buried ice.

4.9 miles. Beacon Hill Road to the east ascends to the crest of the moraine at 211 feet.

4.9-5.6 miles. West Side Road descends the proximal slope of the moraine through topography with numerous kettle ponds, including Rodman Pond and Betty Pucky Pond, and kames to the intersection with Champlins Road. The kettles north and south of Swede Hill are dry. In the gravel pit north of Swede Hill ice-contact outwash gravels also show collapse structures. Sandy Hill, a glacial ridge to the northwest presents a ninety foot high erosional face of sliding sands and gravel derived from the underlying outwash and flow till. The beds are folded downward into a broad U-shape and are laced with small, high-angle faults which are probably the result of collapse. The deposit may have originated as an ice-contact feature, perhaps a kame or a channel fill. Sandy Hill provides a virtual navigation beacon for east-bound sailors.

5.6 miles. Turn left (northwestward) on to Champlins Road. Follow the gravel road over hummocky glacial topography of kames and kettles and the small drumlins of the late Wisconsinan readvance. Take time to photograph the scenic views of Great Salt Pond. Surface deposits are granitic, characteristic of their northwest provenance.

5.9-6.4 miles. Views to the north (right) toward the Coast Guard Station and Block Island Sound take in a photogenic hillslope with a stone wall descending over hummocky topography, a kettle pond, and marshland out toward Cormorant Cove and the Coast Guard Station on Harbor Neck. In the view, the channel into Great Salt Pond cuts between two drumlins, Harbor Neck and Gunners Hill. The houses to the northwest are built among sand dunes with occasional small knobs of moraine (probably small drumlins) poking through. Charleston Beach beyond the dunes is accreting north and west due to the northward longshore current transporting sands eroded from Sandy Hill and the bluffs to the south. The beach has grown nearly one third of a mile along the south side of the jetty since its construction in the 1890's.

6.4 miles. Note the sharp contact of glacial deposits with the dunes. The roadbed goes from gravel to dune sand, and then it crosses a filled causeway over beach deposits.

<u>6.6 miles</u>. Looking to the right across Great Salt Pond, you can see the profile of the Corn Neck Moraine in relief against the skyline, reminiscent of the traverse of Corn Neck made in Highway Excursion 3. The distal slope to the south outlines the drumlin shape of the ridge at Indian Head Neck. The land elevation increases gradually northward to the crest of the recessional moraine.

<u>6.8 miles</u>. The road ends at the Coast Guard Station. Surficial glacial deposits of the drumlins are probably meltout tills, surrounded by recent beach sediments. At low tide, a large erratic sticks out of the water in Cormorant Cove near the southeast point. To the northeast, the marsh and the old, 17th century, breachway area lie on the other side of Gunners Hill.

BEACH EXCURSIONS

WEST BEACH EXCURSION. Gunners Hill north to Sandy Point and south to Settlers Rock, 3.2 miles (Figure 24). This walk takes you from the channel into Great Salt Pond past eroded bluffs of the Gunners Hill drumlin, across a

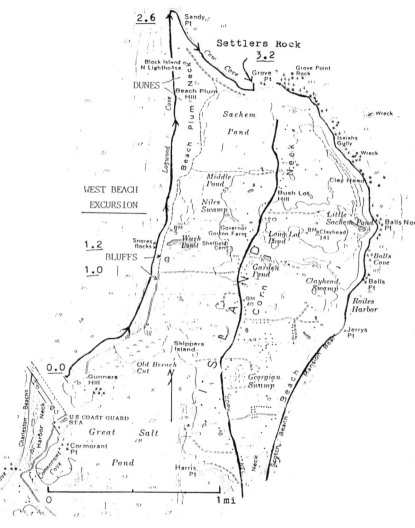

Figure 24. West Beach Excursion. Gunners Hill to Settlers Rock.

tombolo that has been breached frequently by storms and washovers, into a topography of an accreting beach and dunes. Remnants of the 17th century breach, reopened in the 18th century, still exist as shown on the map. Check your location with reference to local landmarks and topography. This beach is heavily populated by shore birds that nest and lay their eggs in the gravel. Please walk along the intertidal zone wherever possible and proceed carefully over the berm to view outcrops of glacial deposits and dunes. Access to the starting point can be by the west end of West Beach Road and a walk to the south on the beach

0.0 miles. Start north on the beach at the north jetty of the channel. On the northwest side of the Gunners Hill drumlin, wave erosion has cut a small scarp in meltout till.

0.6 miles. The glacial drift is buried by coastal dunes up to ten feet above sea level. To the south the old breachway through the barrier is flanked by washovers of sand. These sand bodies were carried across the barrier by storm surges. Divers have found submerged peat beds northwest of this beach; the peats attest to the erosion and beachward (eastward) migration of the tombolo, which was originally deposited over the coastal marsh.

0.9 miles. The twenty foot high bluff west of the end of West Beach Road has eight feet of dune overlying a wave-cut bench on four feet of loess. This sits above upper drift meltout till which contains granitic boulders (Figure 25). A peaty paleosol has formed on the loess.

1.0 miles. Adjacent to the west end of West Beach Road. Two bluffs west of the transfer station fence reveal both the lower and upper drift sheets. In the southerly bluff, the wave cut bench is on the lower drift (the loess appears to have been eroded away) rising to about two feet above the high tide line. The lower drift is overlain by rip-ups of lower drift in the younger outwash and more than five feet of meltout till.

1.2 miles. West of Wash Pond. In the northerly exposure, there are up to six feet of lower drift of which the upper two feet are oxidized to a reddish hue. The lower drift is capped by about eight feet of meltout till with boulders, and at the top, a one foot-high sand dune.

1.2-2.6 miles. North of Wash Pond, the ridges immediately to the east are all coastal dunes that formed on a terrace of glacial deposits. The presence of

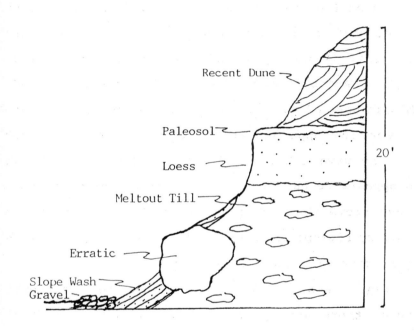

Figure 25. Geology of the twenty-foot bluff, West Beach.

glacial sediments below the dunes is indicated by the thick beach gravels, which are the erosional remnants of the drift. At least one of the dunes appears to have a water plane at about its midpoint. This perched water may be the source of a spring once used for fresh water by early lighthouse keepers. The beach along Beach Plum Neck is steep with coarse gravel berms. The gravel extends up to and around Sandy Point above the high tide line. Large blowouts (wind excavations) in the dunes were initiated during various construction projects around the lighthouse, and then made worse by hikers, four wheeled vehicles and more wind erosion. A visit to the restored North Lighthouse, either as a detour on this walk or on a separate outing, is recommended.

3.2 miles. Cow Cove to Settlers Rock. On the east side of Sandy Point, the beach gravels become finer grained. They coarsen again near Settlers Rock. These gravel berms are cusped. This excursion connects with the Northeast Beach Excursion at Grove Point.

NORTHEAST BEACH EXCURSION. Cow Cove to Mansion Beach (Jerrys Point), 2.2 miles, via Clay Head and Balls Point (Figure 26). This walk along a beach below the high

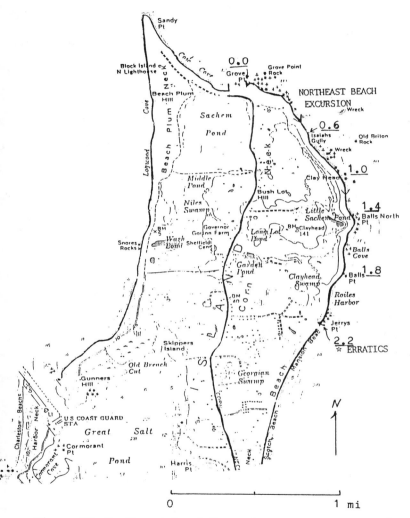

Figure 26. Northeast Beach Excursion. Cow Cove to Mansion Beach.

bluffs of the northeast coast is highlighted by a view of the outcrop of a thick wedge of deltaic sands that were deposited over the upper and lower glacial drifts. Here we see various exposures of lower drift covered by upper drift outwash and meltout till with the deltaic sands above the till. The delta was deposited by a stream draining the glacier into a proglacial lake that formed where meltwater was hemmed in between the retreating glacier and the moraine. Note that the outwash and the lower drift were deformed by the advance of the last glacier. The delta typically has three distinct sets of beds: coarse, stream-deposited sand and gravel (much like outwash) at the top, steeper sloping sand layers at the front of the delta where it lies below water level, and fine silt and clay beds that may form varves on the lake floor. All of these sediments were derived from the wasting ice.

<u>0.0 miles</u>. Start at the east end of Cow Cove near Grove Point. Beach gravels coarsen toward Grove Point, the first low bluff and the source of the rock debris. The clusters of erratics on the beach and offshore illustrate the long-term erosion and recession of the bluffs.

0.1 miles. In the bluff at Grove Point about three feet of meltout till covers up to five feet of lower drift exposed at beach level. To the southeast, outwash grades laterally into coarse sand, medium sand and then clay in the bluff below the old cottage.

0.4 miles. The coarse sand to clay succession represents the beds of the delta and defines the position of a proglacial lake (Figure 27). Southward, crudely stratified meltout till increases in thickness to over thirty feet, and marks the position of the ice margin just before the lake formed.

Erosion at the top of the bluff has cut into a postglacial peat bog and chunks of peat have fallen to the beach. Farther down the beach, similar peat beds have been analyzed. The peat contains spruce pollen deposited twelve thousand five hundred years ago.

Southward, the meltout till thins and the outwash thickens to over thirty feet and contains flow till, a type of till often found bedded in the outwash.

0.6 miles. At the point north of Isaiahs Gully, ten to fifteen feet of fine-grained deltaic beds overlie twenty feet of outwash.

0.75 miles. In the cove at Isaiahs Gully, a mass of

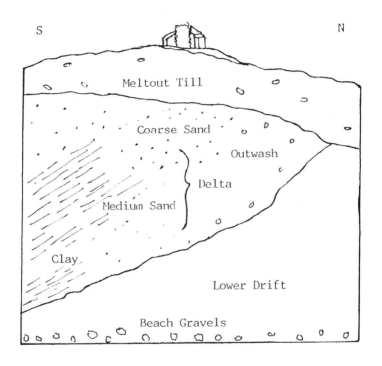

Figure 27a. A geologic section characteristic of deltaic beds as exposed in the northeast bluffs.

Figure 27b. Deltaic beds in the northeast bluffs.

white Cretaceous clay with lignite protrudes from the bluff below deltaic beds. Similar clay and lignite beds have been analyzed from Clay Head and the coastal bluff east of Spring Street. Pollen in the lignite indicate an age equivalent to the Upper Cretaceous, Raritan Formation of New Jersey and Long Island.

1.05 miles. At Clay Head, the clays can be of lower drift, proglacial lake bottom or Cretaceous origin. They have been largely eroded away leaving iron oxide-cemented outwash and deltaic beds. Look for "Indian paint pot" concretions on the beach. These began as rounded, red-colored nodules of iron-cemented sand surrounding a ball of clay in the Cretaceous sediments and increased to a few inches in diameter through deposition of additional iron oxide. When cracked open, they become hollow vessels suitable for mixing paint from iron oxide pigment and clay, a practice attributed to the early residents of the Island. To the south a section of contorted sands and flow tills reflect ice movement and deformation of its deposits. Observe the gullying of the bluffs, the overhanging of soil layers at the top, surface vegetation riding slump blocks down to the beach, water seeps, sand slides and cones of sand at the bottom of some gullies.

These features illustrate the relentless wearing away of the bluffs by the elements and the continued slope adjustments due to gravity. Midway along this bluff, massive slides of the deltaic sands cover large parts of the cliff face.

1.35 miles. Balls North Point. A thick layer of outwash emerges beneath meltout till. The outwash grades southward into nearly forty feet of deltaic sands below bouldery meltout till.

1.55 miles. White sands, either Cretaceous in origin or sand colored by eroded Cretaceous clays, appear at the base of deltaic sands.

1.70 miles. Approaching Balls Point. The geology in the bluffs in the vicinity of this Point is complex and of rapidly changing configuration due to numerous thrust blocks of Cretaceous sediment and lower drift. In general, loess covers the bluffs, and meltout till and outwash thicken and engulf masses of contorted lower drift. Successive exposures show meltout till of the upper drift above lower till which has been eroded into hoodoos. These are oddly-shaped, erosional remnants of till. There are numerous iron-cemented layers in the lower drift and in the overlying outwash. A wedge of deltaic sand also appears above lower till, and thick, bouldery upper till. The fine-grained loess contains numerous bank swallow nests, small circular holes bored into the sediment. The loess is the easiest material for the birds to excavate, and it retains the cylindrical shape of the nest.

1.8 miles. Balls Point. In this sixty foot bluff, upper meltout till and outwash and lower till appear to dip steeply northward giving the impression of a high angle fault or a north-tilted block abutting lower drift to the north. However, erosion has revealed that the lower drift north of the fault is a thrust block engulfed in outwash and partly covered by slumps in the core of a south-trending thrusted fold (Figure 28). A wedge of deltaic sand also appears over the lower till and thick bouldery upper till. Masses of white Cretaceous gravel protrude from the bluff at beach level.

South of Balls Point, several iron oxide-cemented groundwater channels, known as pipes for their resemblance to water pipes, stand out at beach level. The largest pipe has been called "Pots and Kettles" after the iron oxide crusts that coat the cobbles contained in the pipe. This outcrop has been substantially reduced by

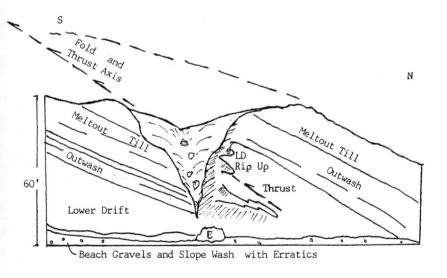

Figure 28a. Geologic section along the bluff at Balls
Point.

Figure 28b. The Pots and Kettles iron-cemented beds.

Figure 28c. Detail of Pots and Kettles cobbles and matrix.

recent coastal storm erosion that has also revealed the continuity of the outwash layer in which the pipe formed. To the south, the lower drift thickens below meltout till and deltaic beds. Look for granitic erratics on the beach and offshore.

2.0 miles. Roiles Harbor. The bluffs are lower in elevation and composed mainly of loess and granitic meltout till over deformed lower drift. In the cove, sand dunes and alluvium cover peat and lake deposits. The loess below the dunes has a paleosol profile. Analysis of a once thicker exposure of the peat bog (now eroded away) identified spruce pollen in twelve thousand five hundred year old peat, evidence of postglacial spruce forests and cold climate at that time.

2.2 miles. Jerrys Point and Mansion Beach. Note erratics at the Point and cuspate gravel berms on the beach. Connects with the Crescent Beach Excursion.

CRESCENT BEACH EXCURSION. Mansion Beach (Jerrys Point) to Old Harbor, 2.3 miles (Figure 29). Here the bluff-dominated coastline of the Northeast Beach can be compared with the Crescent Beach barrier, its dunes and headlands.

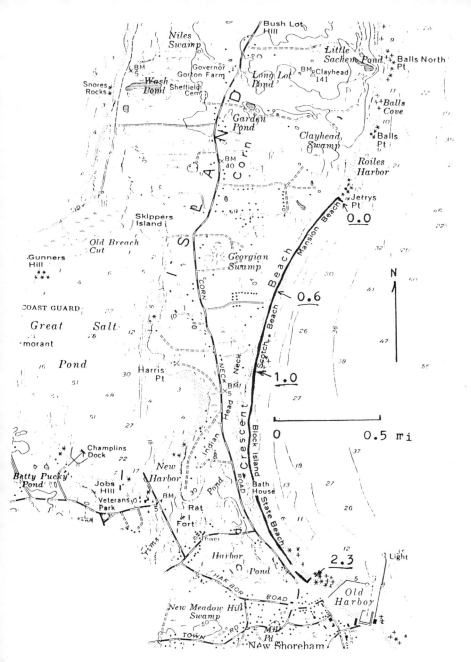

Figure 29. Crescent Beach Excursion. Mansion Beach to Old
Harbor.

0.0 miles. With the offshore erratics at Jerrys Point behind you and the Mansion Beach dunes to the west, proceed southward along the beach. Note the scenic farm on the drumlin to the west. In the spring, the beach is formed of deeply cusped gravel berms. These may be covered with a sand sheet in mid-summer. If sea level was three feet higher here, how far inland would the high tide line intersect the land surface? Low dunes now protect the back beach, but these dunes have been eroding at a rate of about one foot per year, with much of the dune erosion due to trampling by beach enthusiasts. In the absence of the dunes, where will the sea intersect the Island? Do you think that new bluffs will be carved into the hillslopes?

0.6 miles. The bluffs rise above the beach and are a constant source of beach nourishment, that is, they replenish the sand eroded from the beach. The gravels and erratics here lag behind the erosion of the sand.

0.9-1.0 miles. The first bluff sections show lower till below sand dunes. A low, wave cut bench with a thin loess cover overlies ten feet of upper meltout till and lower till.

1.0 miles. Southward, iron-stained outwash over lower

till grades to four feet of crudely stratified meltout till and cross-bedded outwash sands above the lower till. In the higher bluffs just north of Scotch Beach, the meltout till and outwash thicken. Large angular and contorted rip-ups of lower till lie above lower drift at the base of the bluff (Figure 30). Bank swallows have carved their nests into the firm loess stratum at the top.

1.2 miles. In the succeeding lower bluff, meltout till over lower till grade into a loess-capped bench. Recent vintage sand dunes cover the loess.

1.3-2.3 miles. The beach is dominated by sands, with a sand berm and a line of primary dunes up to twenty feet above sea level to the west. The dunes are heavily eroded by paths and blowouts. Glacial drift is at a shallow depth below the beach as indicated by traces of gravel and patches of heavy mineral sand. These sands, weathered from the glacial gravel, thicken near the Town bath house where drift has been exposed after beach erosion and the dune sands have been redistributed. In the past, these mineral sands, which are rich in iron-bearing minerals, have been used as refractory sands, for making the molds used in metal castings, blotting sands,

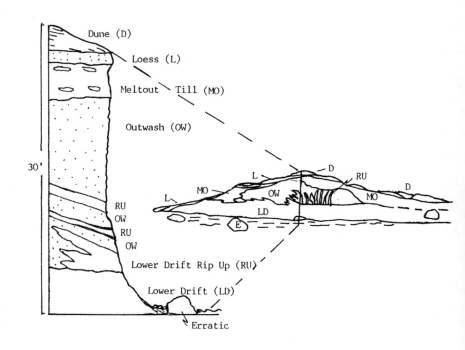

Figure 30. Geologic section and column of the Scotch Beach bluff.

which were used to dry liquid writing ink before blotting paper was invented, and as a source of iron during the 17th and 18th centuries. The garnets in the sand are specific to certain rock formations on the mainland, and can be used for studies of provenance of the drift.

Note that the Town Bath House and the openings to the north and south replace the primary dune. With this break in the dunes, the parking lot collects washovers and wind blown sand during the winter. To the south of the bath house, bouldery riprap and piles of debris bordering the causeway are meant to promote deposition of sand and stabilize the embankment. Dredged sand from Old Harbor channel has occasionally been dumped on this beach. This fine sand temporarily nourishes the beach, but it is quickly eroded by the waves.

2.3 miles. Old Harbor

SOUTHEAST BLUFFS EXCURSION. Mohegan Bluffs to Great Point, 1.0 miles (Figure 31).

0.0 to 1.0 miles. Although only one mile in length, this portion of the southern margin of the Island presents complex and rapidly changing geology along a line across the grain of glacial flow and thrusting. Start on the

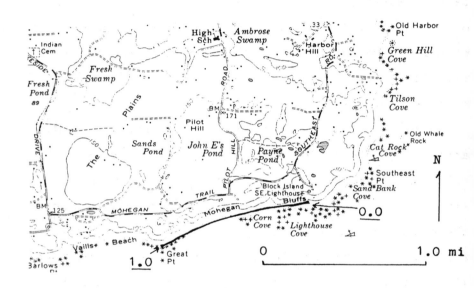

Figure 31. Southeast Bluffs Excursion. Mohegan Bluffs to
Great Point.

bluff north of the stairway. Observe the geology of the bluff below the Southeast Lighthouse, where deeply gullied, slumped, detached and eroded blocks of lower drift tower above the coarse gravels of the beach berms. Light-colored and sandy upper drift covers the lower drift (Figure 32). Here a deep salient behind the pinnacles, or hoodoos, cuts toward the lighthouse and reveals a bluff of highly deformed drift mantled by erratic boulders.

Descend the stairs to the beach. Check the erratics ahead on the beach for composition. Most are granitic, but a few dark-colored gneisses can be identified. A stream has cut a deep channel west (left as you look at the bluff) of the stairway. Take a moment to listen to the clatter of the cobble gravel in the surf. Turn east (left as you face the water) to see the gullied and slumped bluffs from the level of the beach.

To the west of the stairs, both the upper and lower drift units can be seen in the bluffs. The light-colored upper drift with its granitic gravel overlies masses of lower drift. Thrusted blocks of yellowish Cretaceous sandy clay contain lignite. Lower drift hoodoos form a pattern of spires, ridges and detached slump blocks

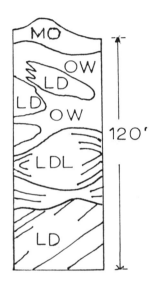

Figure 32a. Generalized geology of the Southeast Bluffs: Upper drift meltout till (MO) overlies upper drift outwash (OW) which incorporates masses of lower drift (LD) and lenses of folded, lower drift lake beds (LDL), all of which overlie lower drift (LD) in place.

Figure 32b. The geology of Mohegan Bluffs. Note the deeply gullied lower drift below and the horizontal upper drift layers near the surface.

jutting from the cliff.

Again to the west, iron-stained outwash surrounds masses of lower drift. As you walk along the south shore, you can see a bedded sand unit dominating the bluff section at beach level. These beds are contorted into tight folds. Thin silt and sand layers engulf detached blocks of lower till comprised of chaotically deformed clays. These clays may have been deposited on a lake bottom. Meltwater channels cut into the bluffs are filled with bouldery rubble.

<u>0.9 miles</u>. East of Great Point, sandy layers, dark clays, sands with gravel, and thin-bedded flow tills are common.

<u>1.0 miles</u>. At Great Point, masses of lower till are surrounded by highly deformed, sandy outwash, and overlain by meltout till, with iron-cemented zones in both outwash and till.

Note the modern geologic processes at work along the beach: mud, clay, sand and debris slides; active slump blocks; alluvial fans of sand in gullies; and wave cut benches at the water's edge.

RODMAN HOLLOW TRAVERSE. Rodman Hollow to Black Rock Point 1.1 miles (Figure 33). Here is an opportunity to explore the topography and glacial deposits of the Rodman Hollow meltwater channel. Dense vegetation and steep slopes add to the challenge of this excursion. While it is less than one mile as the crow flies from the entrance at Cooneymus Road to the bluffs, the Rodman Hollow trail curves into the meltwater channel and around its western side, before rising westward onto a high meadow overlook. **0,0-1.0 miles.** From the top, observe the depth of the valley and the steepness of the valley walls. The upper surface reveals granitic deposits, possibly meltout till. Initially engulfed in shrubs, the trail soon turns to the left into the depression, then to the right over granitic outwash gravel. The land becomes open where the trail divides at a signpost. The left fork traverses a slope of granitic gravel and offers views of the trail head upslope toward Cooneymus Road, as well as the slopes of the channel walls.

At the next signpost and stone wall ascend the slope; there is more granitic gravel under foot. A stone wall follows the slope into a depression. The trail winds north and then west, passes a signpost and then

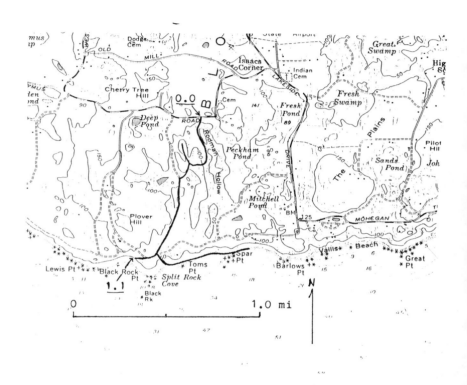

Figure 33a. Rodman Hollow Traverse. Rodman Hollow to
Black Rock Point.

Figure 33b. Erosion of a meltwater channel where it intersects the bluffs along the south coast, south of Rodman Hollow. Note the cobble gravel in the meltwater channel and the lag deposit of cobbles on the beach.

opens onto morainal topography. Ascend to the overlook across a ridge of granitic gravel, passing a kettle to the west. The trail passes a stone wall, numerous large erratics and a signpost pointing toward Black Rock Road. Note the granitic gravel indicating passage over surficial deposits of upper drift.

To the south, the Atlantic Ocean and the south end of the meltwater channel at the coast are visible as you descend the glacial terrain. The trail cuts across a closed, dry kettle (a pond did not form here because the bottom of the kettle was not sealed by fine sediment) and ascends a slope with granitic pebbles. It then intersects a dirt road, Black Rock Road. Turn left and follow the road downhill, noting granitic gravel in road banks. You will see a slight increase in dark-colored stones as you go further downhill.

Go through the intersection with the next lane and continue straight to the top of the bluff. Turn right and follow the road as it turns into a path that ascends the bluff to an overlook of the cliffs and ocean. The bluff here is capped by a sand dune about eight feet tall.

1.1 miles. Black Rock Point. Return to road, turn

left, then right and follow the trail to the beach. Here the bluff has a thick lower till unit, with iron-cemented zones, overlain by thin upper outwash.

To the east below the first cottage, thick lower drift abuts contorted deltaic sands below upper outwash beds. The next two headlands to the east are supported by thick and contorted silts and clays of probable proglacial lake origin. On the beach the increasing proportion of dark-colored stones indicates a lower drift source. Upper drift meltout till covers these lower drift deposits. Note the coarse-grained, granitic boulder rubble set into the bluff at Split Rock Cove (Figure 33b).

GLOSSARY

Advance, Glacial. Movement of glacial ice, radiating out from a center of ice accumulation, down a mountain valley into lower elevations, or over a continental land mass, into lower latitude terrain.

Amphibolite. A type of rock, usually metamorphic, comprised mainly of iron, magnesium silicate minerals, such as hornblende, and plagioclase feldspar.

Aquifer. A porous and permeable layer of rock or sediment capable of readily transmitting groundwater.

Avalanche. see soil flow.

Back Beach. The area of the beach landward of the berm.

Barrier Beach. An elongate, offshore sandbar complex that is deposited parallel to the shoreline and in the down-current direction. Barriers may isolate river mouths to form bays or lagoons.

Basalt. A fine-grained igneous rock, basic in chemistry, composed of plagioclase feldspar and iron, magnesium silicate minerals.

Basaltic. Rocks in the basalt group or having a composition similar to basalt.

Basal Till. A compact, dense variety of till found in

the base of glaciers or deposited beneath the ice. See also lodgement till.

Batholith. A mountain-sized, igneous intrusion often formed in continental crust above subduction zones due to high heat flow associated with crustal plate collisions.

Beach. A seaward sloping, shoreside plain, often sediment covered.

Beach Cusp. See cuspate berm.

Beach Face. Seaward sloping portion of the beach plain in the tidal zone.

Bench. A relatively level erosion plane above the surrounding land surface, often forming a low platform above sea level where associated with coastal erosion.

Berm. On a beach it is a relatively level, but raised depositional ridge at the high tide level of a beach face; it marks the division between the forebeach, beach face and the back beach areas.

Blowout. An erosion hollow formed on or among dunes or open ground by prevailing winds.

Bog. A wetland often with a thick accumulation of peat below a swampy, vegetated surface.

Bottomset Beds. See Delta.

Cenozoic Era. The most recent of the major divisions of

geologic time, divided into the Tertiary and Quaternary periods.

Coastal Plain. A relatively flat or gently sloping plain of layered sedimentary strata that generally merges with the continental shelf.

Cobbles. Small, rounded rock fragments, ranging from about three inches to twelve inches, and larger than gravel and smaller than boulders.

Collapse Structures. See ice-contact structures.

Concretion. A nodular mass of locally-formed compacted or encrusted sediment, generally incorporated in sedimentary strata of similar age but contrasting grain size.

Conglomerate. Sedimentary rock composed of coarse, rounded rock fragments in a finer-grained matrix.

Continent. A major landmass, often comprising a single crustal plate along with the adjoining oceanic crust.

Continental Shelf. Subsea margin of the continent.

Country Rock. Existing bedrock; may be host to igneous intrusions, and subject to regional metamorphism.

Crescent Beach. An arc-shaped beach formed as a sand bar or infilling of an embayment, and connecting two headlands.

Cretaceous. The third and last geologic period of the Mesozoic Era; the rock units formed during that time.

Crust. The outer layer of the earth; it is segmented into plates which carry continents and ocean basins.

Crustal Plate. A division of the earth's crust; one of a number of major and minor continental and oceanic crustal segments bounded by adjacent plates.

Cuspate Berm. A series of crescentic troughs carved into a berm's linear form into crescentic troughs by the action of wave sets. Beach cusps.

Debris Flow. see soil flow.

Delta. A landform resulting from sediment from a stream or river deposited in a larger body of water like a lake or an ocean. Deltas typically have a triangular shape and are made of three sets of sedimentary beds: the top set representing deposits of streams; the foreset formed on the sloping face of the delta below water level; and the bottom set beds made up of fine sediments that settle to the floor of the lake.

Deposition. The process of laying down sedimentary material by running water, currents, waves, wind, and glaciers.

Distal Slope. Slope of a moraine facing away from the

glacier.

Drift Sheet. Glacial deposits associated with a given glaciation.

Drumlin, Drumlin-Shaped Hill. A glacially streamlined, oval-shaped hill often resulting from glacial advance over older glacial deposits or erodable bedrock.

Dune. A hill of wind-blown sand; a sand deposit bearing distinctive gently sloping windward layers and steep sloping downwind beds.

Dune Ripple. Miniature dune forms in parallel ridges covering a sand dune.

End Moraine. The moraine deposited at the farthest advance of a given glacier or glacial readvance.

Epoch. A subdivision of a geologic period.

Era. A major subdivision of geologic time.

Erosion. The process of removing and transporting materials through the action of wind, running water, glaciation, waves and shore currents.

Erratics. Cobbles and boulders transported, usually by ice, from their source areas into regions of dissimilar material.

Escarpment. A more or less continuous cliff formed by erosion or faulting. Also called scarps.

Fault. A fracture in bedrock or sedimentary layers along which there is relative displacement of the two sides.

Feldspar. A group of common, rock-forming aluminum silicate minerals.

Ferromagnesian. Term generally applied to rocks rich in iron, magnesium silicate minerals like amphiboles and pyroxenes.

Fetch. Direction from which waves are propagated by winds blowing over open water.

Flow Till. Till washed intact as a mass of sediment from wasting glacial ice, and often deposited interlayered with outwash.

Foliation. Lamination resulting from the segregation of light and dark minerals in metamorphic rock.

Forebeach. The area of the beach seaward of the berm.

Foreset Beds. See Delta.

Glacial. Features and conditions characteristic of glaciers.

Glacial Advance. See Advance, Glacial.

Glacial Deformation. Reorganization of masses of sediment, including older and contemporaneous glacial deposits by glacial movement. Material may be shoved, faulted, folded, picked up, carried and redeposited or reorganized by advancing ice, or let down, slumped or collapsed due to melting of supporting ice.

Glacial Drift. Sediment carried or deposited by a glacier.

Glacial Lake. A body of water resulting directly from glacial melting. It may be impounded between a glacier and adjacent bedrock or glacial deposits, or it may occupy glaciated terrane. See Proglacial Lake.

Glacial Lobe. A regional extension of a portion of an ice front, often directionally controlled by the underlying topography and its geologic structure.

Glacial Readvance. Renewed forward movement of the ice, usually due to climatic cooling and the resulting increase in the accumulation of snow and ice on the glacier; sometimes due to internal dynamics of the ice mass. Often involves ice shove and causes reorganization and sculpture of existing deposits.

Glacial Recession. Wasting of an ice sheet usually due to climatic warming. Results when melting of the ice exceeds resupply of snow causing the retreat of the ice margin and thinning of the ice mass.

Glacial Stage. A major interval of glaciation within a glacial epoch.

Glacial Stand. Temporary state of equilibrium of the ice front in which movement is static.

Glacier. An accumulated mass of ice formed in a mountain valley or in a polar land area from snow compacted under pressure of its own weight. The ice mass is often large enough to occupy a regional land area. As the ice thickens it may flow laterally or down grade.

Gneiss. A foliated (with mineral grain laminations) metamorphic rock in which mineral grains are large enough to be identified without magnification. The grains are arranged in light and dark mineral bands.

Gondwana. The southern hemisphere supercontinent of the early Paleozoic and post-rifting Mesozoic eras comprised of continental plates ancestral to Africa, South America, India, Australia, and Antarctica.

Granite. A medium-grained igneous rock of acidic chemistry, made of quartz, feldspar, mica and other accessory minerals.

Granite Gneiss. A gneiss in which the foliations are comprised of granitic minerals, often closely resembles granite, but with conspicuous banding.

Granitic. Pertaining to granite; often relating to rocks of continental origin.

Groundwater. Water that has infiltrated the soil, bedrock or aquifer, forming an unsaturated zone separated from a water saturated zone by a water table.

Groundwater Divide. Subsurface topographic or structural high from which groundwater flows.

Groundwater Reservoir. An aquifer or zone of groundwater saturation in bedrock or sediments.

Groundwater Surface. The upper boundary of the zone of groundwater saturation; the water table.

Gullying. Formation of small, deep erosion channels by running water.

Holocene. The current geologic epoch, dating from 10,000 years ago; also called the Recent Epoch.

Hoodoos. Pillars and spires that are the erosional remnants of compact sediment layers, such as lodgement till.

Horizon. A distinctive, thin bed or surface.

Hummocky Topography. The irregular surface of glacial moraines with hills (knobs or kames) and depressions (kettles).

Ice Contact Structures. Deformed deposits of glacial sediment adjacent to the ice, with the bedding offset by faulting due to ice shove or collapse when ice buried below the deposits melts out.

Ice Front.   The down-ice extremity of a glacier.

Ice Margin.   The temporarily stable, regional extremity of a glacial front resulting from the balance between the resupply of snow to the glacier and its melting and flow.

Igneous Intrusion.   Upward movement of molten rock into existing bedrock from a magma chamber below.

Igneous Rock.   A type of rock formed from the cooling and crystallization of molten rock (magma).

Illinoian Glacial Stage.   The third of four major glacial stages of the Pleistocene Epoch.

Interglacial.   The interval between glacial stages.

Interstadial.   A warm interval between ice advances within a glacial stage.

Indian Paint Pot.   A rock-like vessel or concretion that formed due to iron oxide deposition around a clay filling.   Used as a paint pot by some native people.

Inverted Topography.   Topography in which a geological feature, normally of depressed relief, such as lake beds, is elevated above the surface.

Iron-Cemented Zone.   Channelized area in sedimentary layers or soils in which iron compounds are deposited in the form of pipes, lenses or zones.

Island Arc. A chain of islands, usually volcanic in origin.

Island Arc-Basin Complex. A volcanic island arc and the depositional basins adjacent to it, similar to the Islands of Japan and the Sea of Japan.

Isotope. Any of two or more forms of the same element, having the same or closely related properties and the same atomic numbers but different atomic weights.

Kame. An ice-contact conical hill of stratified outwash deposited by water flowing off the ice or into a crack in the ice.

Kame Delta. Similar to a kame, but deposited as a delta into standing water adjacent to the ice.

Kame and Kettle Topography. Hummocky morainal topography containing kames (the hills) and kettles (the depressions).

Kettle. A depression formed in glacial drift by the melting of a remnant block of ice.

Kettle Lake. A lake formed in a kettle; usually the base of the depression is sealed by fine sediment allowing water to collect.

Lag Deposit. Coarse-grained rock fragments remaining after fine-grained materials have been eroded away.

Laurasia. The northern hemisphere supercontinent of the early Paleozoic, incorporating continental blocks ancestral to North America, Europe and Asia.

Lava. Molten rock from inside the earth that reaches the surface through faults, fissures, rifts and volcanoes.

Lava Flow. A layer of molten rock that covers the surface.

Leachate. A liquid that flows down through some material; can refer to the polluted liquids that drain from a landfill.

Lens. A body or layer of material that is thicker in the middle and tapered at its edges.

Lignite. A brown to black, soft coal.

Littoral Drift. See Longshore Current.

Lodgement Till. Till deposited under a glacier and compressed and compacted by the weight and movement of the ice.

Loess. Silt winnowed from recessional glacial deposits by wind blowing off the ice. The silt is deposited downwind in thick structureless, homogeneous layers.

Longshore Current, Longshore Drift. Current generated by the direction of waves against the shoreline that transports sediment down current and parallel to the shore.

Magma. Molten rock beneath the earth's surface.

Mantle. The layer of the earth between the crust and the core. It consists of peridotite, rock denser than basalt.

Meltout Till. Till deposited during wasting of the glacier, often of a stony texture with some of the fine sediment washed away.

Meltwater Channel. A channel cut by glacial meltwater, usually into glacial sediments, and extending outward from an ice margin.

Mesozoic Era. The major division of geologic time between the Paleozoic and Cenozoic eras; represented by three periods, the Triassic, Jurassic, and Cretaceous.

Metaconglomerate. A metamorphosed conglomerate in which some recrystallization of the matrix has taken place and rock fragments have been sheared and stretched.

Metamorphic Rock. A type of rock resulting from the chemical and physical alteration of existing igneous, sedimentary or metamorphic rock by heat, pressure and chemical change. It involves recrystallization and growth of minerals, compaction and the creation of shear planes or foliations.

Mica. A group of common, rock-forming silicate minerals that can be physically split into thin plates.

Mid-Wisconsinan. A reference time for events happening between early and late Wisconsinan glaciations; may be applied to a warm interval centered around 30,000 years ago.

Moraine. A linear ridge of sediment deposited by a glacier.

Morainal Topography. Pertaining to the surface of a moraine, which is usually irregular and often characterized as kame and kettle or hummocky topography.

Mud Flow. See Soil Flow.

Obduction. During plate collision, fragments of the descending plate may attach to the upper or overriding plate.

Outwash. Layered sediments, usually sand and gravel, transported and deposited by glacial meltwater away from the glacial front.

Outwash Plain. Outwash from a glacier may form a broad plain adjacent to the glacial margin or end moraine.

Paleosol. A soil horizon, surviving from a prior interval, that has been buried by younger sediments.

Paleozoic Era. The major division of geologic time

before the Mesozoic Era and after the Proterozoic Era; includes geologic periods from Cambrian to Permian.

Pangaea. The ultimate supercontinent of the late Paleozoic and early Mesozoic eras, made up of all known land masses that joined during the early and mid-Paleozoic. Pangaea began to break up at the end of the Triassic Period; its fragments comprise the present continents.

Peat. Organic sediment made of the partially decomposed remains of wetland plants, compacted and chemically altered in a bog.

Peat Bog. Bogs form in wetlands where layers of peat accumulate.

Pegmatite. A rock type, usually of granitic composition, characterized by very large crystals, which result from slow crystal growth from cool magmatic solutions. Minerals include quartz, feldspar, mica, and rare minerals.

Perched water table. The groundwater surface formed in strata above an impermeable layer which lies above a regional water table.

Peridotite. A general name for the denser, iron, magnesium silicate rich rock, composed of olivine and pyroxene minerals and believed to be characteristic of the earth's mantle.

Period. The major geologic time units of an era.

Permafrost. A zone of permanent ice or frozen ground at or near the surface of the earth.

Permeable. The characteristic of rock and sediment layers that enables fluids to flow through their interconnected open spaces.

Phyllite. A low grade metamorphic rock, similar to slate but with a sheen due to the growth of microscopic, platy minerals like mica.

Pipe. A grounwater conduit, often cemented by iron oxide to form a continuous tube-like structure.

Piping. The tendency for groundwater to form channels in sedimentary layers. Redeposition of iron oxide on the walls of these channels forms pipe-like structures.

Plagioclase Feldspar. A related group of common rock forming minerals composed of sodium, calcium, aluminum silicates, and having very similar physical properties.

Plate. See Crustal Plate.

Plate Tectonics. The processes associated with the interaction of the earth's crustal plates. The processes include plate collisions, mountain building, subduction of oceanic plates, rifting, and development of island arcs and depositional basins.

Pleistocene Epoch. The older of the two epochs of the Quaternary Period, 10,000 to 2 million years ago (the Holocene, 0-10,000 years ago, is the younger epoch); an interval of cyclic glacial and interglacial stages.

Plume. The extent of seepage of leachate into the subsurface strata; also applies to upwellings of mantle rock on convection currents.

Podzol. Soil with an organic mat, a leached A zone and a B zone enriched in iron and aluminum, and developed under forests in cool, moist climate (also Spodosol,Pedalfer).

Pollen Zones. A means of synthesizing data derived from the abundance of fossil pollen as assemblages of pollen of various plant types in sequential sediments. The zones approximate the general vegetation at a given level or time of sediment deposition from the ratio of pollen types. In Quaternary sediments, such as lake and marine clays, bog peat, and paleosols, pollen zones are useful for reconstructing pre- and postglacial vegetation and climate; postglacial pollen zones range from the Herb Pollen Zone representing tundra vegetation and cold climate, through the Spruce Pollen Zone, Pine Pollen Zone, to the Holocene Oak Pollen Zone.

Pore Space. Open space between mineral grains in sediment or rock. Connected pore spaces allow fluids to move through the material (permeability).

Porous, Porosity. The characteristic of sediments or rock units that have pore spaces.

Portwashingtonian Warm Interval. A mid-Wisconsinan Stage warm episode named after the geographic location of the characteristic deposits on northwestern Long Island, New York.

Precambrian. The four billion years of geologic time before the Cambrian Period, the earliest period of the Paleozoic Era (beginning 590 million years ago).

Precambrian Shield. The relatively stable, ancient continental crust of precambrian age that forms the core of a continent.

Proglacial Lake. A lake that forms adjacent to a glacier, often confined by the ice front, valley walls and moraines.

Proterozoic Era. The major division of geologic time before the Paleozoic Era.

Provenance. The source rock or terrain as revealed by

rock or mineral types in transported sediment.

Proximal Slope. The slope of a moraine facing the glacier (the opposite of distal slope).

Pyroxene. A group of common, iron and magnesium silicate rock forming minerals.

Quartz. A common rock forming mineral; the hardest common mineral, a constituent of granite, and composed of silicon dioxide.

Quartzite. Term applied to rock types made of the mineral quartz. These include the metamorphic variety of the mineral, often found in veins or fracture fillings in bedrock; metamorphosed sandstone in which the quartz grains are fused; and relatively pure, quartz sandstone.

Quaternary. The youngest and current period of the Cenozoic Era, 0 - 2 million years ago (after the Tertiary Period). It is comprised of two epochs, the Pleistocene and the Holocene.

Quick Clay. Water-saturated clays that are mobilized by some type of disturbance. See Soil Flow.

Radiocarbon Dating. A method of determining the absolute age (up to about 40,000 years ago) of earth materials bearing radioactive carbon (carbon 14) using the decay rate of this isotope.

Recent. The youngest epoch of the Quaternary Period and of geologic time, dating from 10,000 years ago. See Holocene.

Recessional Moraine. Moraine formed during a temporary stand of the ice front in the overall process of glacial retreat.

Recessional Topography. Characteristic landforms created during glacial retreat through melting, deposition and erosion. It includes such features as kames, kame deltas, lake deltas, drumlins, kettles, moraines, meltwater channels, and outwash plains.

Ridge and Swale Topography. A depositional surface characterized by parallel depositional ridges and eroded shallow depressions.

Rift. A regional fault running parallel to the regional structure, such as a plate boundary.

Rift Basin. A down-thrown or tilted crustal segment parallel to a boundary rift in which water and sediment may collect.

Rift Valley. Similar to or synonymous with a rift basin, but linear and often bounded by two parallel faults.

Rip-Ups. Pieces of underlying bedrock or sediment layers detached and thrusted by overriding forces, such as glacial ice. The detached and thrusted materials may be thrusted up or into overlying or younger materials.

Rotational Plane. A plane of weakness, usually curved, that develops in rock materials due to stress from erosion, water infiltration and saturation. It may form a zone of potential slope failure that isolates a slump block from the main body of sediment. Small offsets or sags may appear at the top of the plane. See Sag Ponds, Escarpment.

Sag Ponds. Ponds that form in the hollow or depression formed between slump blocks and the main body of sediment (Sags), usually above the rotational plane.

Sand Spit. A sand bar attached to a headland at one end and extended by longshore currents into or across a body of water, such as a bay or river mouth.

Sandstone. A sedimentary rock made of layers of sand deposited on flat or gently sloping surface, and compacted and cemented usually by silica, iron oxide or calcium carbonate.

Sangamon Interglacial Stage. The prolonged warm interval between the Illinoian and Wisconsinan Glacial Stages; believed to have been warmer than the present with higher sea levels.

Scarp. See Escarpment.

Schist. A metamorphic rock in which mineral growth develops a type of foliation in which platy minerals, like micas, are aligned in parallel planes and are readily identifiable.

Sea Level. The average or mean level of the sea over a given interval of time.

Sea Level Rise. A relative increase in the mean level of the sea over time; often associated with climatic warming and melting of glacial ice or tectonic submergence of the coast.

Sedimentary Rock. A type of rock formed of rock debris, such as gravel, sand, silt, and clay, chemically precipitated sediment, such as calcite, and biological materials, such as marine shells. The materials are usually sorted in grain size by transporting currents, deposited in layers, compacted by overburdening sediment, and cemented by mineral compounds.

Serpentine. A common metamorphic rock-forming mineral composed of magnesium silicate and usually of a greenish color.

Serpentinite. A metamorphic rock made up of serpentine minerals; may be the result of metamorphism of basalt.

Slate. A fine-grained metamorphic rock with cleavage planes.

Slump Block. A unit or mass of rock or sediment on a slope that has begun to move along a rotational fault or water-lubricated sediment layer.

Soil Flow. A generalized term for rapid downslope movement of the soil layer, and may be defined as Debris Flow, Mud Flow, Quick Clay, Rock Slide or Avalanche (with ice), depending on the nature of the materials. See Solifluction.

Soil Zones. Distinct layers or horizons of soil development, each with distinct characteristics, like the B soil zone, the zone of accumulation.

Sole-Source Aquifer. An aquifer with only one source of water, usually rainfall.

Solifluction. Soil flow after melting of frozen ground.

Spodosol. See Podzol.

Stade, Stadial. Pertains to the time represented by a glaciation.

Stage. A geologic time subdivision of an epoch.

Stratum, Strata. A bed, or beds, of sediment or sedimentary rock.

Subduction Zone. The crustal region of plate collision

where heavier crust, like oceanic crust, descends into the earth's interior, while lighter crust, like continental crust, overides the descending plate.

Swale. A long, narrow and shallow depression on level terrain between two ridges.

Terminal Moraine. The moraine deposited at the farthest advance of the ice during a glacial stage.

Terrace. An eroded, step-like bench that breaks the continuity of a slope.

Thrust Block. A mass of rock material moved laterally or along a low angle fault.

Thrusting. The process of rock units or masses of rock moving at low angles over existing bedrock due to horizontal pressure.

Till. A deposit of sediment derived directly from a glacier, that is generally unsorted and unstratified rock debris.

Tombolo. A sand bar connecting an island to the mainland or a larger island; in a double tombolo, two parellel sand bars, one on either side, connect the land areas.

Topset Beds. See Delta.

Triassic Period. The initial period of the Mesozoic Era, known for the initiation of continental rift basins, red sedimentary rocks and basaltic lavas filling basins, associated with the beginning of rifting apart of Pangaea.

Uranium-Series Dating. A method of determining the absolute age of material containing radioactive uranium. The age is calculated from the ratio of uranium compared to lead in crystalline minerals from bedrock or certain marine shells.

Varve. A pair of sedimentary layers deposited in a body of water, such as a glacial lake, during a one year cycle. The sand layer represents summer deposition and the clay layer, winter deposition.

Vein. A tabular, usually narrow, intrusion of igneous rock into the bedrock.

Washover. The overrunning of beaches and other landforms near sea level by waves due to storm surge or earthquake wave-driven seas.

Water Table. See groundwater surface.

Wave-cut Terrace. An extended bedrock platform distinctly related to wave erosion; often uplifted or exposed above sea level by a relative lowering of sea level.

Weathering. The geologic process of mechanical

disintegration or chemical decomposition of rock constituents.

Wind Ripples. See Dune Ripples.

Wisconsinan Glacial Stage. The youngest of the glacial stages of the Pleistocene Epoch.

Zone. A band of earth materials with distinctive characteristics.

ACKNOWLEDGEMENTS

The author gratefully acknowledges the editorial contributions of William K. Healy, as well as Mr. Healy's cover design. He also thanks Judy FitzGibbon for field testing several excursions and for the color scheme on the cover.

INDEX